BLOOD & TEARS

Poems for Matthew Shepard

BLOOD & TEARS

Poems for Matthew Shepard

Edited by Scott Gibson

Painted Leaf Press
New York City

Published in the United States by Painted Leaf Press P.O.Box 2480 Times Square Station NY, NY 10108-2480. Printed in Canada.

Cover design: James Maszle.
Cover photograph by: Elaine Angelopoulos
Book design: Brian Brunius

ACKNOWLEDGEMENTS
"At The Inn" by John Ashbery from *Shadow Train* by John Ashbery (New York: Viking, 1981). Copyright © 1980, 1981 by John Ashbery. Reprinted by permission of Georges Borchardt, Inc., for the author. "[Pin Dots]" by Star Black from *Waterworn* (New York: A Gathering of the Tribes, 1995). "Recognition" by Rafael Campo from *Diva* (Duke University Press, 1999). "By gray dampy weather" by Norma Cole from *Desire & Its Double* by Norma Cole (California: Instress, 1998). "And Then I Saw" by Alfred Corn was previously published in the *American Poetry Review.* "Caption" by Peter Gizzi was previously published in *Artificial Heart* (Burning Deck, 1998). "Sheltered by womanhood and middle age" by Marilyn Hacker was first published in *Prairie Schooner.* "Laramie, Wyoming, 1998" by Walter Holland was previously published in *Bay Windows* in 1998. "From rue Wilson Monday" by Anselm Hollo first published in *Sniper Logic* (Boulder, CO Spring, 1999. [Annual magazine of the U of C Creative Writing Program]. "Waste Not" by Joan Larkin reprinted from *Cold River* (Painted Leaf Press, 1998). Copyright © 1997 by Joan Larkin. "Pavane" by David Trinidad is from *Pavane* (Sherwood Press, 1981). Copyright © 1981 by David Trinidad. Reprinted by permission of the author. "Oya/St. Therese" by Emanuel Xavier taken from *Pier Queen* (© 1997 by Emanuel Xavier for Pier Queen Productions).

Library of Congress Cataloging-in-Publication Data

Blood & tears: commemorative poems for Matthew Shepard / edited by Scott Gibson
    ISBN 1-891305-15-8 (alk.paper)
      1. American poetry--20th century. 2. Shepard, Matthew Poetry.
  I. Shepard, Matthew. II. Gibson, Scott. III. Title: Blood and tears
  PS615.B57   1999
  811'.54080351--dc21   99-13126
                                                CIP

PHOTO: Elaine Angelopoulos © 1998

CONTENTS

Introduction

"... [When Matthew Shepard was found tied to a fence] his head had been covered in blood except for a clean spot 'where he'd been crying and the tears went down his face.'"

—*New York Times,* November 21, 1998

This book is dedicated to Matthew Shepard. He was a victim of hatred, and it is impossible for any feeling person not to be touched by his death. We are diminished as a people by his loss, and how we respond will indicate our own advancement as a society, a culture and a nation.

The poets included in this book offer their responses in a variety of voices. Their poems and accompanying letters are evidence of the difficulties they have faced maneuvering among the complex of emotions that erupt as a result of such a heinous crime—rage, sorrow, frustration, fear and even the possibility of hope. Some of the poems are new, while others, written previously, have been submitted in Matthew's honor and memory.

Ultimately, what happened to Matthew is everyone's nightmare. This book is a reminder of what happens when hatred and violence combine. In that spirit, a percentage of the profits will be donated to a national anti-violence organization.

I wish to thank Michaela Kahn, Lisa Jarnot, Linda Eastlund, and my mother, Jan Michael, for their help and support, and I extend my gratitude to everyone at The Naropa Institute's Jack Kerouac School of Disembodied Poetics.

Scott Gibson

BLOOD & TEARS

Poems for Matthew Shepard

A Circle Lighter Than Air

George Albon

Matthew Shepard 1976-1998

Paper thin / razor

thin. Tolerance no contract
but a smoldering wait.

"Young man setting forth,"
narrative, strange weather.

If the safe passage
were open structures,
large meadow, any sky.

The thugs drink from the pond,
brains smooth as a billiard ball.

To find the light shines the way
from the brutal village.
To find it.

Lorca takes our friend
taken from us
and his own midst,

holds him, tells
him *I would*
have come between, the

world's shape filling
itself in, put path

and orbit back into
your hands,

I would have stood in their way,

but I had met them already.

At The Inn

John Ashbery

It was me here. Though. And whether this
Be rebus or me now, the way the grass is planted—
Red stretching far out to the horizon—
Surely prevails now. I shall return in the dark and be seen,

Be led to my own room by well-intentioned hands,
Placed in a box with a lid whose underside is dark
So as to grow, and shall grow
Taller than plumes out on the ocean,

Grazing historically. And shall see
The end of much learning, and other things
Out of control and it ends too soon, before hanging up.
So, laying his cheek against the dresser's wooden one,

He died making up stories, the ones
Not every child wanted to listen to.
And for a while it seemed that the road back
Was a track bombarded by stubble like a snow.

Gravity

Susan Baran

*Upon hearing the details of Matthew Shepard's death, I was once again filled with the
same shock and disbelief that had earlier inspired the elegy, "Gravity."*

For William Fener

Billy's dead.
All birds have the same form
but differ much
in size and shape of parts.

Billy's dead.
His '69 Pontiac motored through Canada, Tennessee, the Skyline Drive.
Migrating flocks follow river valleys,
coastlines, mountain chains.

Billy's dead.
Impossible to overfeed
fledglings—their throats
refuse to work when sated.

Billy's dead.
Birds' hearts beat twice
as fast as humans.
They can be near or farsighted at will.

Billy's dead.
"Cheerily, cheerily, cheer up,"
calls the robin. Lighthouses lure
unlucky flocks to their deaths.

Billy's dead.
The hollow bones of birds
support great weight.
Fate waits to bake sparrows in a pie.

Billy's dead.
Pure white eggs laid
in dark places. Judge
the blue jay by deeds alone.

Billy's dead.
Its tail is a rudder
to guide flight and landings.
He plunged ahead without instrumentation.

Billy's dead.
I can't get it into my head.
Birds' bills may be trowels, chisels, augers.
Billy's dead.

Sonnet: For Matthew

V. Barnhart

It is no consolation that you will never have to wait for him to call,
and that when he does call, because he always does eventually,
    there will be no one to answer the phone.
For you there will be no nights after dinner, dancing to some radio station
Laughing and confused, wildly uncomfortable, because you're both leading
    and then both following, until you both stand still and listen.
You will never have to put away his boots, and his shoes, and wash the
    dishes swearing that you're going to kick his ass, only to find that
    he made the bed.
You won't gently push him in the parking lot until it turns into pretend
    Kung Fu fighting, and then somebody slaps somebody too hard up
    against the head and an angry laughing chase leads you through a
    park where it ends with a kiss behind a tree.
His dog will never bite you because she's jealous.
You won't stand side by side, bare-chested, looking in the same mirror
    both thinking how much you hate shaving, both not shaving for a week.
You will never have to sit around, bored and restless, wondering if you're
    really loved.
You won't have those years of wondering together about the crushing
    heart-break of vanity and all the years of narcissism that allowed for the
    peaceful smile to engage your face as you remove one of his own grey
    hairs from the lapel of his jacket.
You will never have memories of that time in Mexico.
You will never remember for the rest of your life, of which you have none,
    the way your eyes really did meet that night, December 13th, a
    million years ago.

So I promise you, at least once in the seconds before I scream out
through a rasping, stifled choke, and before he utters that lowest
earth-touching moan,
That I will think of you, Matthew, and pray for safe passage back,
into gayness in your next life.

...as true of martyrs...

Mark Bibbins

(an Internet cento)

a credit card and a pair of black patent-leather shoes

More to the point, death is not an appropriate consequence for an
       unwanted flirtation. If it were, how many heterosexual men
       might not be alive today?

the butt of a pistol
the Equality State

premeditated malice
protected by the 1st Amendment

Some people in Laramie went so far as to claim that the basket of
       memorial flowers had been arranged on the fence just to
       enhance the cover of *Time.*

gay murder suspects
gay attack
police attack gay march

a modified view of morality
godhatesfags
described variously as resembling a scarecrow or Jesus

All gays must die

I love Sally

these offenses are more heinous than others
all life is precious
It's been an absolutely horrendous year

The 700 Club sometimes with Pat Robertson—they're constantly
        talking about gays.

Comfort Inn: "Hate and Violence Is Not Our Way of Life"
Arby's: "Hate and Violence Are Not Wyoming Values 5 Regulars $5.95"

[Pin Dots]

Star Black

Names with less syllables than mine will lift
cracked stairwells from tenements and broom
them off, add a balcony or two for flimsied
clothespins only the welfare'd use, and replace

them, while the national endowment's moneymen,
without saying anything aloud, baseball-bat more
gays, censor snipping naughty bedrooms, bad art.
Nothing is ever exact. Animals are not precise,

caved in clans on the Sheetrocked millenniums,
huddled above small hungry flames in furs of
the sacrificed. We firefly through a multitude

of these hollows, bringing tiny illuminations
that never stay in one cave long enough to die,
but pass in a bleariness that alerts the eye.

In Remembrance of Matthew Shepard

Robin Blaser

How sad I am. How sad
this violation of the existential
given and Matthew's song—
another debt of this indecent
century—what is to be said
about this *hideous traffic*
in religion that has taught
blasphemy for centuries
against Jews, blacks, aboriginals,
women, Gypsies, and homosexuals
everywhere. "They" put on Jesus-shoes.
He never wore them.
"Their" *sacrifices to hate and hell.*
There is no more to be said
about God, except the *infinite exposure*
of our finitude that "they" have taught.
Love arrives as a promise.
Every particular love is Love,
dear Matthew. How love shatters
when they stopped your song—
the shatters in which we trust.
Yes, the philosopher said: *The glorious body*
cannot but be the mortal body itself.
What changes are not the things but their limits.
It is as if there hovered over them something
like a halo, a glory. Dear Matthew.

Political Funeral in Black & White, What Can I Do?

Lee Ann Brown

I was walking way East on Houston
the other grey day
and saw wheat pasted flyers
for Matthew Shepard's
Political Funeral
on the silver phone poles and
they were starting to peel off in the wind
and I thought I should take a picture
of them for this poem
but when I came back they were
gone or covered by others

What can I do about this now?
Nothing to photograph, to prove
they were there

There were pictures in the paper of people being arrested,
shoved on NYC buses at Matthew Shepard's Political Funeral
attended by many many more people than anyone expected
What can I do about this now?

I can think of him
I can write this poem
Etched into all our skins are the descriptions
we read—of his body and what they did to it
once read they may be covered
over but they will remain etched into us our skins We are

changed and must change We must other our lives
how   how   how   how could this happen
we all know how it happened   even though we want to deny
it's still like this we know this could happen again

Someone by accident or design put a sign over Essex Street
and now it's Sex Street We all live on the Sex Street one way or another
so
Let Everyone Build and Live in the House of their Own Lovely
Desiring Design on Sex Street Openly If We Are To Remain Human We
Must Love the Visit of Neighbors like us or Unlike No One is the Same
When will People Stop This Killing off of Feeling Unspeakable
Remember Again

In Memoriam Matthew Shepard

Reed Bye

We just got back from leaving off a mouse
caught last night and kept inside a box
lined with grass and an apple from our tree.
It sprung out in the fields by Cottonwood trail.
Afterwards as L. and G. and I walked along
the sunny road beside the ditch I thought
about the difference between anger and outrage
in response to flagrant acts of cruelty or injustice:
How anger clashing with its own ignorance (prejudice)
intensifies, so battle lines stay drawn
and deepen. But wiser Outrage in a seasoned fury
reveals horrified ignorance to itself, and so
dispels it (over time) in purifying blasts.
I think of M.L.K., Mandela, and Ahmad.
These thoughts come up in wake of Matthew Shepard's
brutal murder. Little mind
intent on eliminating that which seems to hem it in
with shadows of feared difference, intent on staying small.
May anger grow to Outrage in response
and all our minds enlighten from this darkness.

Recognition

Rafael Campo

That night, while he was beaten, I was stretched
in sleep beside the man I love. I'd dreamed
like anybody does; my heart half-leapt
when I awoke to singing in the shower.
The semi-darkness promised to grow true;

it seemed that life was good, your voice like grace.
As unaware as I was, you were happy.
We fixed our breakfast as we always do.
I toasted bread, too mindful of the hour,
our dog beneath me thinking she's a puppy,

pushing her nose against me, begging treats.
While tears washed blood in streaks from off his face
before the muted dawn, I watched you grind
our coffee, spilling some like dirt across
the green Formica countertop. It felt

like joy, to watch your squint-eyed measuring—
two cups, not more, of glinting water in
the clear glass pot. The simple ritual
that marries light and liquid, elements
that somehow join us—then, you smiled, as if

to prove us safe, or that the trees outside
could recognize us. Somewhere else, the boy
lost hope. A bit annoyed, I wiped the grounds

you always leave behind; by then, they'd found
what first was taken for an animal

that hunters lashed against a barbed-wire fence.
We drove together to the hospital
and held each other's hands, as usual,
bracing ourselves for others' misery,
or maybe nothing in particular,

or something else we'd yet to learn to see.
The boy was dying, rushed by ambulance
across a stretch of frozen countryside.
You kissed me sneakily on going up,
our elevator empty but for us;

your love, I felt, was rising into me.
But later, when we learned with disbelief
how Matthew Shepard died from injuries
he suffered as a consequence of this
same love, I wondered whether I deserved

to die that way, incomprehensibly
as why you couldn't hold me while you cried;
I wondered whether he had touched us as
he left an unfamiliar world, and whether
what he found was anything like grace.

How It Is

Tom Carey

Love how
his hand holds the rail,
how that space becomes
because he has occupied it.
That hand, pink and brown;
an odd thumb.
It's nothing:
Just a brass thingamajig
in front of the bar,
something to block glasses,
except that now it holds
some of his heat.
Ever notice how skin
changes with the light,
or that there's a roughness here
and nowhere else?
Everything he does is interesting
to me, more than interesting:
Everything he does is him.
And what I want,
what I want,
is his diving into me, catching
and holding me up. The world
is like water.
He will do my breathing for me,
and I'll swallow.

Resistance

Abigail Child

for Matthew Shepard

1.

Writ so tightly bounder that Italianate had been difficult, and that his headdress had been cover girl in blooded except for a clean spotted fever where head count been cryohydrated.

The perserverate poundage upon us their real price.

We were beatup in a mannish horror. Thickening would then stun about like giantism, without any will-o-wisp of their own, until the deadbeat came when they quill passant awestruck.

The facial angle distraught by a violinist's urochord as if caryatid in storage cruelly called when the pepper-and-self torpedoed and baksheeshed to death were beginners for destroy.

2.

completely severed having from upper
wrists that difficult rope
harrassed, treading glass
and men
upon

face
with pain
face distorted face
bottom, themselves would like
head in cuts   beaten   prey

3.

Memory undertakes anything
Accompanies the pins in rotation for the
Tenor who beheads the voiceover
To linger and wait close by, or
How, one half of which is
Endowed with nervous jitters
Whether in a person or character of a
Solution, psychologically inappropriate
Hand-to-mourh readiness, a combination of forces
Equilibrium with song, loosely
Physiognomy of a people, the breakup of
Axis, start
Rolling
Disorderly mowers, large in number, unmounted

Meet what speech or is thought to be
Attrition, an attribute designating a unit
Tearful, sexually indulge in
Threnody for a lightskin,
Heal regarded
Example, a waste to inhabit violence
Weep remarkable pounds, to

Set in motion
Heteroclite, wide, broad
Evening stare or
Plain motion to deprive evil's
Alloy, a person swiftly and rapidly
Ringing with lips and ringing on
Daily baited begging (drops)

Motive a nerve and heavier
America with eyespots
Treasure including the remedy for poison
Tail in mouth
High sounds
Enclose a portable head with protracted wants
Wound soreness. enlist gulf
Supporting each
Having more reflective brightness
Elements with one
Pica, vital
Anti, or
Regenerative, thick, wreathe wrapped
Difficult to cut (bound)

two poems:

John Chinworth

snow

in Casper
 dusts the spires
  of St. Mark's
   fortress

cold air
 like the breath
  of a thief
   being caught

stained glass
 freezes blue
  the saints
   in their stories

wildflowers
 just a few
  like a bouquet
   on a fence

25 X 98

french horn

of the hunter
   dogs after the fox
      crimson jackets

open the gates
   for the arrival
      of the prince

Ganymede
   to Jupiter
      - swept skyward

12 XII 98

Allow Yourself To Be Touched

Toria Angelyn Clark

in memory of Matthew Shepard

"Not that I want to be a god or a hero.
Just to change into a tree, grow for ages,
not hurt anyone."   ~Czeslaw Milosz

indisputable, the ground and
the earth know we are equal
allow yourself there
at the heart and here in the air
to be touched

the sky forms coastlines of hope
owl and meadowlark
both choose the highest post
sharing the same tears when
a green leaf is stolen

you may fall apart floating
waves and waves of leaves
limbs laving allow seeping
into earth damp enough from
mother's weeping

allow yourself to be the big trees
alone and yet together in
rings and rings of story

cottonwood and oak
breathe in equal ascension

after all the leaves have fallen
the trunk remains naked
and alive roots sink
deep tangled like faith
an ancient accumulation

Poem

Marc Cohen

It's April
(or it was then)
and some thoughts
follow you wherever you go
so you keep moving
to stay in one place.
Mother said that he kept looking
at his hands.
Maybe he thought
they had betrayed him.
Like the blue jay
(first frozen, then paralyzed by

a yellowjacket's repeated stings)
with its eyes wide open
watching
the masterful hornet
commit murder,
hasten its own demise—
the fatal buzzing no longer exists
as if the building leaped from the man
and loving him would have to be enough.
Mother said she knew him
but what did she know?
April's white smoke rising.
The sound of departing voices.

By gray dampy weather

Norma Cole

By gray dampy weather
The dunes and the seacats
The atmosphere by its density
The slowness re-enacted
Slower moves particular

"like fog holds light"

contents of the box: pale green light; pins; blood; spent shells and a
shot nickel; padlocks, locked; a rope trick with the key at the end of it;
red paint; straight pins scattered among the loose tiles; an Uzi on the wall,
blood on the floor

"we sat right there
and drank all night"

re-experienced
the sleep of reason
considers progression
gives you a sample
"is round"

You have one name when you are here, a different name when you are
        not here.

please keep
this talk
so the ocean
she said
reversing the letters
gathers in a name

a nod, a chain of rocks, a step across
and up the slope to the new school

for Jesse
for Matthew Shepard

AND THEN I SAW

Alfred Corn

Remembering Matthew Shepard

My body, laid out on a marble slab.
Naked but for a linen sheet tucked under
Its chin, as though to keep the patient warm.

A solemn band approached; identified
The late departed with what looked like mingled
Relief, mild satisfaction, and bereavement.

One of them took away an arm—the right,
Was it?—and loped off with a spring in his step.
Which prompted others to do likewise: here

A shoulder (suitable for crying on),
there a foot, there an eye and there an ear.
Plump already, one scooped out the belly.

Just who you'd imagine claimed the head.
Not the one I hoped tugged loose a rib.
Some, by no means all, I knew as friends;

But felt no bitterness, instead, acceptance.
This, while watching their several withdrawals,
Travelers moving farther out and deeper

Into the sunset distance; who all began
To flourish, somehow more intently themselves
Than they had earlier resolved to be.

Was glad of that, despite a fit of shivers
(Simple human nature still presiding)
When I took note of the rummage that remained,

Wishing a greener plot had been marked out
For what had breathed with so much spark and promise.
My turn, then, to come forward for a closer

Look; and, since no one else had carried off
That steady, flexibly strung pump at rest
Beneath the sternum, take it for my own,

Sensing its mute but anchored trust that parts
Lucky for others would befriend as well—
Oh love—even the heir that flesh once named.

Anatomy

Rikki Ducornet

This is how a bone looks when it breaks.
A complex fracture. His hair bright with ice.
The simple body. The extravagant, the subtle body.
> Above:
> the slow moon.

What is scattered there?
It is the sound of a broken vessel spilling water.
This is how a piece of paper is ripped apart.
> Beneath the moon:
> the slower road.

And this is how the body receives the night:
a perfect stranger enters into the dream
to take sudden hold of the heart.
> And now:
> the sudden heart.

Matthew

kari edwards

at first
a day later
filler on the late night local news
gay male assaulted
strung up crucifix style
left to die

now stilld
this silhouette
lays in shadowd silence
on cotton sheet death bed

fast forward days of prayer
they say no news is good news
I never believed them

so little was said by the press until he was dead

why did they wait for death to proclaim outrage

they must know the silence is killing us

in silence we kill ourselves

in silence dragged behind a pickup truck

in silence raped by police with nightstick broom handle

in silence paramedics let her die afraid to give mouth-to-mouth
    resuscitation

in silence he was outed by police, raped, reported it, then murdered
    by hir assailants

in silence they were all taken in isolation

in silence my fear is never far away

in silence they all rest eternally in my tears

hir is a gender neutral pronoun

SEEKING TENDERNESS

Beatrix Gates

The bird instead
incites us
to recall our future.
>>~Claribel Alegría from "Merlin" (trans. Darwin Flakoll)

I

Blood cake cowlick
Palms like kleenex
Brow cleaved open
Skull cocked hat.

Deaf to music
Shirt tails billow
Hard October
Birds won't land here.

Bright-seeing silent night.

II

Stories walk backwards
out of the split-rail lodgepole pine,
the deer fence where you hung,
limbs scorched, star-stung, rusty throated
no song:

Once Chastity hid her boyfriend Russell's bloody clothes,
the girlfriends helped make up alibis. They couldn't
decide what to do with Matthew's size 6,
black patent-leather shoes. The wallet
tossed empty on a night table,
the shoes gleamed in the trailer's corridor.
And what would Aaron say
if Kristen admitted she wanted to try them on?
She kept her mouth shut, chewed at the corners
(same as when she said, "they just wanted to beat him up
bad enough to teach him a lesson," talking later to 20/20)
but the black patent-leather shoes glistened,
strange and magnetic like a city, a place she'd never walked,
full of dark mirrors where she could look in
and one minute see the great night sky
and the next, laugh at their small distorted faces leaning over
to study the faggot's favorite shoes
trying to figure out whether to ditch them or not.

Someone said that Aaron, like a lot of people who talk a lot,
had nothing to say, that his friends called him a shrimp,
just bullied him around, put him in a headlock and held him
there. "He wasn't the mean guy,"
one said, "he was just Aaron, the little guy."

When Doc, the limo driver from Doc's Class Act
pulled up in the 25' white Lincoln stretch
Matthew said, "I want you to know right now
I'm gay and we're going to a gay bar. Do you have a problem with that?"
And Doc threw back, "How are you paying?"
laughing as a friendship began. Shepard worried

about splurging on the trip to Fort Collins for an all-nighter
with his friends at Tornado and how badly he wanted to go
where he could dance and swing in another man's arms.
"He would tell you anything," Doc marvelled
about his talks with his new customer.
Doc was friends with another set of regulars,
Aaron and Russell, and had given an apartment
he had in town rent-free to Aaron, Kristen
and their young son.

Now when Doc drives by that stretch of road
accelerating up the bluff a mile east of town,
he sings loud to the radio trying to block the voices
he hears in the wind crying "no-good faggot" and "please, please
don't kill me." Later, he can't help
replaying Matthew:
"If I could get two people who hate each other—
one straight, one gay—to be respectful of each other,
I would have done something good." This is the song
that keeps finding him and he cannot repeat.
He still feels for the two who killed,
so he drives the roads at all hours, slow
then fast, then steady, driving
whoever needs to get somewhere else for whatever reason.
He sits behind the wheel tapping out the hours
against the leather-encased rim,
the blue-dark empty sky in front of him.

"Russell's about the most American
kid you can get. He's a pizza-eating, beer-drinking,
fishing, hunting, work-on-your-car
type of kid—just regular," his landlady said.

Russell's mother, Cindy, was found frozen
1000' from a highway shortly after dawn in the new year.
She was wearing a shirt, jeans and a pink nylon jacket.
The bartender at the Buckhorn Bar had refused
to serve her saying she was too drunk already
and asked her to go stand by the window
to wait for her ride. What did she see?
The tail lights blurring or a big TV
coming closer like the one her husband pushed
her head through? She walked 4 miles that night.
Wind came and carved
her senses awake: too late, she knew
where she was headed, drove her legs
towards the line of hills, the cut of road ahead
until she couldn't face it anymore.
Jacket zipped high around her neck,
she stopped. Wind drove her down
to the hard pan where she lay in the shelter
of the Arctic cold.
Russell said his parents were dead
a Taco Bell co-worker said.
"I didn't even know he had them in town."

III

"Guess what?
I'm not gay and <u>you</u>
just got jacked."

Truck door shut,
Russell pulls out the .357-caliber magnum,
angles the butt of the handle
and begins.

The bicyclist who found Matthew Shepard
thought he was a scarecrow
until he saw the human hair.

Wall of wind
breaks the spine of words.
The heart will not wander
without love's definition.

IV

Later, he will fly,
wrists still bound to the fence,
the wind in back of him
easily lifting him off his feet.
He will fly towards them
as they turn towards home
after a night on the town.

He will be like billowing
clouds that rake the plains
this time of year, change hour to hour, comb the grasses
silver, then red, keep coming.
He will fly, one of a flock of birds
that keeps darkening the sky as they pour

over the plains with the force of water.
He will be flying with grace and purpose
trying out all the angles learned by all those
who have gone before:
how to fly while being dragged
through the hot dirt in Jasper,
Texas at the end of a chain
tied to the bumper of a pickup truck,
or how to sing through the eyes
like the two women lovers looking for a house,
gagged then bound back to back,
who took bullets to the head
in southeastern Oregon.

He will fly because he is hungry
for it, the beautiful mouth of the sky
taking in all he has to give, the tenderness
of beating wings all around him.

12/15/98–1/15/99

UNCHOSEN ROADS

Scott Gibson

Matthew Shepard will be gone again tomorrow
he will teach compassion again, touch
the chests and stomachs of men,
hearts of human beings again, Matthew Shepard
will be a friend again, Matthew Shepard
will make us cry

      They began to cry
      beside Wyoming sunset
      his eyes hardly closed
      face caked with blood, like
      clown make-up and tired
      voice; past begging screams
      by 4 PM that Wednesday
      life's video rewound
      most quickly, his tears
      washed blood under
      thoughts dried white
      beneath Laramie shadows

      They began to cry
      his friends, parents, and we
      who never knew him
      the blood dried
      to our hands and faces

years of silence
as he fought
alone, with two others'
dirty hands sculptured
hate was it, fear
being called a faggot or
banal power over five
feet two inches of
human life

Matthew Shepard will never cry again,
he will never fight for gay rights again
never buy two dollar Corona or tip
fifty percent again, not touch the skin
of a man or flash friendly smiles, Matthew Shepard
will not meet new friends again, not cry
again, he'll never ride in pickups on unchosen
Wyoming roads or be robbed for twenty bucks
and black leather shoes or be beat
in the head by heavy Magnum steel or
tied and hung to a Laramie buck fence again
Matthew Shepard will not cry again, beg for mercy again.
He will not freeze again or grow hair
on his shattered skull or beg for mercy again
he will never be lonely, Matthew Shepard
will never cry again.

CAPTION

Peter Gizzi

One less body is lost in snow
The dying one (in time) becomes a landscape,
     do you remember how it came about?

Snow unlike glass, glass unlike a corpse
Moon unlike a torso boldly colored in
     with bark, with slate, with soil breaking up

in the furrows of another eroding shape

Or a severed line, bringing us together for the first time
March unlike Spring or an almanac out of date,
     nomenclature: everywhere

Evidence, perception, conclusion
Unlike a dull pool on a brown tire track,
     earlier I said landscape

How did it come about?

Grief unlike truth, truth unlike snow
Body unlike its outline

THE GUILT OF HERCULES

Robert Glück

for Matthew Shepard

I put on my necklace
To make the street mine
Still alive
(

The Cry of the Owl
By Patricia Highsmith
Desk and light
(

Death is unwelcome
In the white noir
I bark like a dog
(

God keep and protect me
From the straight line
(

CLEAN SPOT

John Greyson

Pigs and ducks and geese gonna scurry
When I take you...

ducks and geese gonna...
When I take you out in my pigs and ...

When I gonna...

Proteus (not protease). Sage of the sea who tended the seals of Poseidon.
If his feet remained on the rock, he could change himself into any shape he
pleased. But. If he was seized and lifted, he must foretell the future. And.
If he was seized and lifted. He must die.

scurry...

Peter Grimes: Opera

Lauren Gudath

Anchors sink.
Shoal teacher blames atmosphere.
sing   song comets
        sing about fishing

Everyone outraged.   The outrage sure.
    Everyone sure. Blush for all
        kisses,
        Peter

Time to fire guns
eliminate right from culture.   No cash.
    Anxious in social, no useful, functions.
  Prizes for give great
        burden fair. Fairer boys of merit rare.

Peter thinks poorly—gossips –money—gossips.
    To crush the gossips and marry the widow
        unkill the orphan. The mob wins and
            has the best part. The widow understands; she's
    the anchor knitting body.

Another riveting confession of depravity and cowardice.
    Obscures the obscurity of the obscure. This
        opera poses no threat to destruction.

The pacifists were wrong.

No Nazi is better than no Britten. Or Isherwood. Artists.

We'll always have Wagner to reconsider. And millions

dead forever.   We have Paris too.

Boys. Fragile. Great. Unseen. They fell.

Sheltered by womanhood and middle age

Marilyn Hacker

I.M Matthew Shepard and Dr. Barnett Slepian

Sheltered by womanhood and middle age
from their opinionated ignorance
since I'm their teacher, since they're my students,
I try to wedge bars of their local cage
open... But what they're freed to voice is rage
against every adjacent difference.
The week the boy froze on the barbed-wire fence
a strapping senior roasted "men in drag"
bad attitude, grotesque, arrogant, ugly.
And if some skinny gay kid, black like him
(as Matthew and his torturers all were white)
made an inopportune advance one night,
what would be his righteous masculine
response? Flagellate and crucify?

Who's keen to flagellate and crucify?
The sleek umber young man was more complex
than his predictable gender-and-sex
prejudices. What idea or fantasy
was fleshed for him in Thom Gunn's elegies ?
And the tall blonde girl, her long neck's
chignon a dancer's, in what context
was it revealed to her that *feminazi*
was the word for other young women who

railed against a certain status quo—
jealous, of course, deserving to be *beaten*?
Did she think I might imagine my own arm-bone
splinter as grinning frat boys knocked me down
while I read (with a teacher's distance) what she'd written?

While I read (with a teacher's distance) what she'd written
– her *obersturmführerin*: a lesbian Jew –
I wondered what violence she'd been witness to
or suffered, that she had, or had not, forgotten,
but could not name, that prompted her to threaten
anyone who'd try to tell her, "you
don't have to take that shit." But I withdrew;
something heavier than indifference set in
and neither her fresh grace nor her obvious
pain provided me with the right questions.
In my windowless and anonymous
office painted institutional green, her
awkward plea hid in a trial sestina
behind a slur devised by "right wing Christians."

Behind a slur devised by "right wing Christians"
the battered boy hangs naked on barbed wire;
a picture window shatters in sniper fire:
the obstetrician who performed abortions
bleeds into Sabbath bread.
                                    (That week's distortions
which Pizza Hut evangelists inspired
featured angelic embryos, martyred

by selfish women with degenerate notions.)
In a bare-walled projection-booth-sized room,
the students pass the week's assignment out.
A pile grows on my desk, page upon page,
in which, against the odds, may be a poem,
instead of calumnies from which I'm not
sheltered by womanhood and middle age.

The Fence

Rachel Hadas

Grey sky. Dead grass. Cutting wind. A fence.
No one near.
Simply to be allowed
to share the public air,
to move without fear—
these are the first laws of innocence.
No one to hear.

The women on the wall
cried out at Troy.
The vengeful warrior
ignored their agony,
pursued and caught his prey,
and to finish what he had begun
pierced the dead man's heels
and dragged the body round and round the town
without at all
easing the savage ache in his own heart.

A wife and mother
kills the triumphant warrior, her husband,
who had sacrificed their daughter.
Their son returns from exile
and gathers up his strength
to kill his mother.

Drowsy November afternoon.
My students bend to their blue books and write.
How does justice work?
Punishment? Revenge?
Is one life worth
more than another?
For whose sake do the Furies,
weeping tears of blood,
rise from the ground
and hunt the killer down?

No one to see
whose tears washed two paths
clean on his bloody face,
who stood, wrists bound
(the ropes, a sheriff said,
almost too tight to cut),
tied to a fence under the autumn sky
as night turned into day.
No one nearby.
No one to say
whose enemy he was,
whose prey, and why.

A More Empty Wyoming
or Ad astra, thinking of Matthew Shepard

Griffin Hansbury

Two dollars in my wallet, walking home
down Second Avenue under the faint few stars.
I should spend them on a streetside telescope
peepshow to see cloudy Jupiter,
sexy Saturn and her buttery rings, all
the seemingly small things that spin eternally—
and yet, I get a jug of milk instead (fat free).

A jug of milk assumes I will be here
tomorrow (and the next days) to drink it
in cereal, protein shakes, etcetera. What
an arrogant way to spend a lonely pair
of dollars, when I could have had
those heavenly bodies, the moon, the stars.
Who knows what my last glimpse will be.

In Wyoming the stars are bright as planets,
spilling in their milky way, a billion gallons
trembling with our shared pasts and chemistry.
How indifferent they come streaming to us,
remembering a quieter Earth, a more empty
Wyoming—empty of pistols and pick-up trucks,
empty of boys hung from buck-fences to die,

empty of buck-fences. Wyoming once was filled
only with the gorgeous emptiness of the West,
her state bird and flower (meadowlark,
Indian paintbrush), before there were state
birds and flowers (before there were states)
and state mottoes—Wyoming's being, "Equal Rights."
I won't speak of ironies; there are other mottoes

I'd prefer to put here. North Carolina's, for example:
"While I breathe, I hope." Or flat Kansas
with its pretty Ad astra per aspera,
"To the stars through difficulties." Again,
the stars. The last good thing he looked at,
a glittering view above the plains. At least some
loveliness seen from that vastly difficult dying.
In those last hours of breath (silvered
in the chill), of hope, the bleary stars
must have held some solace: God and the ongoing
going-on of the Universe. The stars in their light
years have known our past, but cannot
tell our future, though the Zodiac will try.
We will not know our last night when it comes.

This one might be mine. Oh, there are boys
(right here in New York City) who would kill me
just as quickly for the way I came crying
into the world, less than usual—or, rather,
I should say more—shining, bloodied,
separate I came. If they could have it
their own brutal way, then: shining, bloodied,

separate I would go. Go where? you ask.
To the stars, of course. Free of the body
with its quenchless wanting, its weeping,
its unwelcome lusts and dull requirements
of money, of milk; free of the body and its breaking,
where would you go? To the stars (it isn't so hard);
to go home, once again, to the welcoming stars.

VIGILANTE

Paul Heiner

Everything in the body will shut down
All at once possibly, eventually, some-
Thing will come over. Hate it when that
Happens to be the root of all minutes—
Bound to be bludgeoned, alive, left like

A scarecrow. Batman is risen, will come
Again to be more clear about it, eye for
An eye-hole in his leather-hooded body-
Suit. He is packing and he will arrive so
Too, he is notoriously buoyant, all that all

Hollow is, just like a cave would be, except
That there are people who actually live there
Readying the cumulus for highfalutin rights.
Pulse-winged, qualm-perfect, red rubber blood.
You rise to dress for getting what you should.

Lament for Matthew Shepard

Gerrit Henry

What to do?
O, what to do?
Where to go
If not to you?

Where to go,
And whom to love?
How imagine
God above?

Why go on,
O, why go on?
When you've already
Come and gone?

When to meet again,
How to say?
When to mourn is to honor,
And to hate is to pray?

Laramie, Wyoming, 1998

Walter Holland

Gay Man Beaten and Left for Dead; 2 Are Charged

(For Matthew Shepard)

His body more as a scarecrow's
hoisted up on the fence like a cross—
eighteen hours to find its redemption.

Who does it scare? Image of flesh and blood,
a boy's figure strung to wood, what do we say
when it's taken down? Primary motive

robbery, but we know the crime is only
hate. Sentinel of that field, out there, you hung
to bring us back to fear and scatter all thoughts of an early

harvest, but we will not run. They are the ones
with minds of straw, the soul-less cloth blown through
by wind, they are the scavengers we rout, by staying visible, by being out.

from *rue Wilson Monday*

Anselm Hollo

32

returns, twilight-summoned, the master of dolorous speak
now click here for dazzling version of nothing
but hearts moated by joyful pessimism
sing with watery creatures, sleep in leaky boats
curtains on eyelids, dark laughter heard falling
out over ivy, with music, cut to tracer bullets
earth trembles under mysterious house on Closed Eyes Road
closed form is coffin, Pentagon is closed form
expensive explosives engulfed by fracturing stone
punctuate swarm of questions, "it's all opaque"
watch the cerebral thermometer disintegrate
globules of mercury, angle of hand on keyboard
sparks of silence & nonsense fly up the chimney
longing: a kind of loitering, with no intent

Todd, Matthew; Matthew, Todd

Yuri Hospodar

Todd, Matthew; Matthew, Todd
10-12-98
Todd B. Hawley my partner, lost to AIDS 7/11/95
Matthew Shepard, murdered by bigots 10/12/98
Todd, take care of him,
Todd take care of him;

You have grown so good at greeting new arrivals:
you helped calm Chris
as he reached your new shore
mere months behind you.
And Dave, too, tired,
needed leaning on you
and you led him to peace.

Your beloved grandmother, ancient, dreaming of Odessa,
surprised no doubt to see you Otherside
first—
for once it was you with stories first to share, and wisdom
to give.

And now, a new emigre
whose end pained the world,
who should have been a success at whatever he did,
but not as this beaten,
bloodied celebrity.

He should have finished school, learned of life, found a job,
forged a career in foreign service, found a man he loved,
vanished comfortably into humanity's horde,
witty and kind at well-planned parties,
caring for his companion in sickness and health,
with his mind aimed toward helping the world he cared for so,
not his skull shattered by a .357 Magnum gun butt—

Matthew trusted them all. He believed in humankind.
Like you, Todd, it's said he had faith in everyone.
He will need to adjust to his last brutal lesson,
that too many claiming life are not humankind.

He is young, so teach him patience,
he will miss so much those yet living he loves,
but tell him (you were always so good at explaining)
Eternity, too, is a kind of time,
and a kinder time,
and all of us who love,
whose hearts have burst
yet somehow beat still,
Here or There,
we will be together,
peaceful, again together,

peaceful
left alone
together
again.

BABY

Kathe Izzo

cry

without softness

your skin is on fire
you do not know cry
yet you know over there
is something
you do not know

fire is your skin
the air cry

stop you do not know
stop or not knowing stop

do you scream (skin)

you are everything (skin)

REQUIEM

Lisa Jarnot

I am thinking of something to remember this by—
a brick thrown through a window, a broken jaw,
a passion, a love, a reciprocity,

      with no attempt to obliterate one or the other,

      with no difference between this man and the next,

the doors to love led by the flickering of a flame,
a plum orchard, a peace-loving nation,
beaten, robbed, stripped, and stabbed,

      the surging waters of the heart

      ecstatic, all encompassing, mindful of death,

that he was thrown over a bridge
and drowned by a group of teenagers,

      that they shut their eyes

      and let him go,

punished by god with hurricanes, with earthquakes,
with meteors, with fire—

      this news from a reliable source,

      this news a simple enumeration of facts,

he was shot in the chest,
he was severely beaten with a blunt object,
he was run off the road,
spray painted on homes, on cars,
on fences, on the sign posts—

      this is a peace-loving nation,

      this news from a reliable source,

that he moved west and decided that he wanted to be the mayor,
shot five times at his desk,

    with this attempt to obliterate the other,

    with this difference between this man and the next,
by one's words, condemned,

    this is a peace-loving nation,

    a garden full of fallen leaves.

My Matthew Shepard Poem

Patricia Spears Jones

My students are rightfully spooked
someone their age was left to perish
because he preferred the company of men.

My mother tells me of seeing a man lynched
back in the 30's, in Arkansas, not far from where
I grew up and grew away in the 60's.

What I know about America is that hatred
crawls through the culture like the cracks
in the San Andreas fault.

Edifices are built to withstand the inevitable
quakes, but the quakes grow stronger.
What ever we dream harmony or a reasonable tolerance
is destroyed in the wake

of men drinking and killing. Their bloodlusted
laughter howling through the night.

A Black man in Texas. A white man in Wyoming.
A doctor at his window about to eat dinner with his family.
A nurse on her way to work at a clinic.

The playing field is not level. In fact, there is no playing field.
There are men enraged by change. And women bitter about it.
And people, say

gay, Black, Latino, Chinese, Japanese, Arab, or Jewish
to blame, always to blame.

The ugly men in their same wool suits and stripe ties
gibber political correctness, freedom and fairness
and fuck you
every time they claim that these are acts of individuals, not of society.
Each act alone represents

singular aberrant behavior, like *murder.*
I can hear them say, I mean they actually lynched that boy,
even as they call this one *faggot* and that one *nigger.*
And they really, really want women
compliant and girlish
or sexless and mothering.

And if this seems like male bashing, so be it.
If the dress shoe fits, may it pinch like hell.

(NEXT) TIME

Michaela Wolf Kahn

we sit on headstones in the parking lot
gold filter at his lips, he's smoking camels again.

tuesday night
he drove home
from the gay bar
took his dog out, went to bed
from a different bar
you were driven
beaten with a pistol butt
strung up   scarecrow
fractured skull against Wyoming buck fence
left to October ice
tiny, torn and
bleeding into death

     I bury my body
     dark bath water
     pretend I am fish
     pretend I don't breathe
     live in warmth of
     candle flicker
     pretend my pulse
     doesn't skip this beat

          these eruptions can't go on much longer
          soon the fever will be sweat

blue eyes
yours a sweet boned face
precious skull
marrow splintered

      pretend I'm safe
      if I never leave the bathroom
      pretend I'm ok if
      I forget and swallow
      enough, once, twice—
      not enough to bandage
      your head Matthew not enough
      to stop the burn and blood

            I bleed and name that blood yours
            sacrificial
            to an earthen altar

we sit on headstones in the parking lot
gold filter to his lips, he's smoking camels again.

I can't watch
the smoke between us
curl off to atmosphere
      can't speak the damp or
      grasp the stone
      can't write the seed
            this vomit
            I won't swallow anymore
            won't watch them beat
            him coming home
            next time

Spread Eagle Ghazal

Meg Kavanagh

Niboowin, Niboowin, I thought I could tell by observing
how your brow skin stretches when your mouth tells lies.

White Matthew Shepard died in Wyoming, tied up
Spread Eagle. Spread Eagle. You know what that means?

My dogs barked at the morning. Your truck pulled into the drive.
Or did my dogs bark at your truck, mud packed in the morning?

An Eagle. Human hands and feet. A clean spot of cheek.
Human hands and feet. Face of a son.

I slept beneath your blanket and caught a fever so crisp
it spoke to the dried wings of dragonflies, called them brother and sister.

THE PHANTOM OF THE OPERA

Kevin Killian

> *Had this been a heterosexual these two boys decided to
> take out and rob, this never would have made the
> national news. Now my son is guilty before he's even
> had a trial.*

His little feet are green.
Take the barrel off the wright
for his green feet. For a load of
chops. Matthew Shepard, 21
Propellor to the stars, the green stars, high over Laramie's
outskirts and weary and back to the base line
the fence on which they found him
a scarecrow

I fell apart when he approached,
a dizzy fog flailing round my skeleton
arms flapping, and used this
to write novels

the beautiful birds this dead boy scared away
the welts forensics took for burns

this weakness—
in intensive care
Nurse figures in transit, and swift about it
Doctor, stat,

have you ever seen feet so green
he's been stepping on clover
a piece of state scum

dunked into a barrel. Boys
said the queen of Minna Street
have you been set upon by thugs

Russell Henderson, 21
Aaron McKinney, 22,
themselves slight,
who robbed you of your underwear

Boys don't forget me
I've your welfare at heart
said the queen of Minna Street
his pale feet in the rug of their scalp

As they walk away
their asses throb like chlorophyll
shrug

A is for Kevin
B is for missed the bus on O'Farrell Street, standing there, my paper and dick
C is for AIDS deaths dropped in half in 1997, now only the 15th killer
        in America
D is for plastic sheets, two men huddle beneath, dancing, performance
        and E is for the night we
saw Louis Malle and Uma Thurman in that restaurant
        and met Kiki Smith

"F," as in Clint Eastwood, hairy stare
      K to the I to the double-L
anagram = Old West action, what do they spell

Matthew Shepard, 105 pounds, five foot two,

"G,"—other causes leap out of the pack
      accident, suicide, murder, sign of the cross
          as AIDS drop down to 15
            after 15 years
and murder in Laramie
      "A" is to axe and "H" is to hatchet
"I" is for "iris" and "J" is for "jacket"
He took a long turn to 405,
kept the cure, his neck burnt black
"J" put the stopper in perfume X
took the wheat from the Blistex bottle
"K" for the almost perceptible slur
in your bankbook, I don't remember half
of these guys, that got key-toned

Exist now as letters only—
alphabet mired in gum
"L" is for Matthew, who sat on a fence, scaring crows,
"M" did the wild thing on my dime

The pop art {George Oppen wrote}—a Disneyland tour of Dadaism? or the
anger, the destructiveness of the homosexual, the totally disconnected, the man without
natural valences—to him not only the structure but the purposes of society
must seem AT ALL MOMENTS totally absurd.

Black plantain cross rosary plate
on snowy white linen
snarled with your drool
so I keep my books in plastic sheets
I am the little boy who went in
          to the sea to rescue your scarf

from misery heap, picked over by
hungry—
and—
It is true, Christine

I am not an Angel, nor
a genius, nor a ghost

I am Erik

Forget the name of the man's voice

the corpses change but the party goes on forever,

NO TEARS FOR QUEERS / NO FAGS IN HEAVEN

Dean Kostos

The speakers throbbed with red music.
       He will fill your mouth with laughter,
       and your lips with shouts of joy.
"What do you want? Where can we take you?"
       He did not create a chaos.
They gunned the engine, wind
whipped black as they sped,
       And ask for the ancient paths where
       the good way lies, and walk in it . . .
passing corn and wheat and barley fields
to a threshing floor:
fists pummeled his frame, fists hammered
a pistol butt into his skull,
jeers stabbed the icy air,
his face collapsing on their rage.
       O prosper the works of your hands.
Arms roped cruciform to a rail,
legs, spread-eagled, he torqued, fell
limp. While the pupil-dark sky loomed
in witness, the light of his body dimmed.
       And all of us, with unveiled eyes, seeing
       the glory of the Lord
       as though reflected in a mirror
       are being transformed into the same image . . .
Breath wheezed through swollen nostrils
and lips, all identity crushed
but his name.
       Protect them, O Lord, in your name. . . .

The title refers to slogans carried outside the church where Matthew Shepard's funeral service was held.

Matthew Shepard

Joanne Kyger

Election Day
        Do you think a vote
   for sexual respect

and tolerance could out voice anger
   and fear   soul wandering

victim of who you are
'the problem is never other people'

unless they kill you
You're a human being, right?
     Such an interminably sad

peace is your death

November 3, 1998

WASTE NOT

Joan Larkin

We're using every bit of your death.
We're making a vise of your mouth's clenching and loosening,
an engine of your labored breathing,
a furnace of your wide-open eyes.

We've reduced you to stock, fed you to the crowd,
banked the pearl of your last anger,
stored the honey of your last smile.

Nothing's left in your mirror,
nothing's floating on your high ceiling.
We're combing pockets, turning sleeves,
shaking out bone and ash,
stripping you down to desire.

Your beloved has folded your house into his—
I'm wading the swift river, balancing on stones.

In the moments before dawn,
Matthew hears a coyote cry

Michael Lassell

Is that a coyote call?
It must be late.
If I could see, I'd lift my head, but
the blood has frozen my eyes shut.
The sound always frightened me before,
the wild yelp that marries a cry
before its dying fall.
Tonight I find it more
like a song
than a howl.
It won't be long.
I'll never last
out here where
Aaron and Russell beat me
for loving men.
The coyotes know I'm going to die
and when.
They seem to care.
They know that presence is comforting;
you isolate
to make
a kill.
Still,
I, too, made the usual human mistake:
full of anger or sadness, maybe hate,
I slandered them, more for being outcast

than for their reasonable appetite.
I should have loved their bark,
my canine sisters, brothers...twins.
The snow is so white
except for the red. And the black
tracks
that break
into a run before disappearing
into the dark.
Once again, the predator wins
by might.
I'll never be kissed
or held close to a heartbeat.
True carnivores hunt on two feet
and carry a fang in each fist.
What really kills is not
the difference between you and me,
but the difference between what
a man is and who he is told he ought
to be
by people who profit from
lies.
Lies.
The bludgeon, like the Bible, is only a prop.
Someday they'll be caught
and brought
to justice.
Perhaps I'll be missed.
I want to be.
Is it the alpha female calling
the charges in her pack?—

Afraid the men have done to them
what they have done to me:
roped me to a fence
and left me alone
to die?
Nothing in nature would believe why
even if we had the language to explain our sins
or the will to atone.
I wish I could answer back.
She seems so overwrought,
as if she needs relief.
At least I'm part of something here,
an icy moment before dawn.
Soon the sun will rise and
I can sleep.
I hope they find me alive—
I've already been devoured by those who
feast
on grief,
and my mother, weeping, will want at least
to touch the thing that was her son.
I wish she didn't need to see
what the lies have done.
If only the pain would stop,
I could die in peace.
If only the lies would stop,
we could live there, too.

2 January 1999

Sonnets to Matthew Shepard

Tony Leuzzi

More than October, the wind connects us.
At night, when I am short of breath, I hear
The whistle from its spiteful tongue speak loss
To skeletons of flowers. Loss and fear—
Hours pass like seasons. And I'm left thinking
Everything in Autumn dies, even you
White waif of the violent west, Wyoming's
Son who simply was: who? I wonder, who!
Had you not been anonymous, would I now
Endure the truth of our ill-fated congruence?
Parallel pathways of desire? And how
All inroads lead me to the same difference?
Red sky, night rings hollow like the crow's caw.
Diminished last, thought, is this what you saw?

Maybe the night never came. While you dreamt
Another dreadful hour in a clearing
The cold air baptized you in its vastness.
The symbol of your death has always been
Here, walking the branch of a naked tree
Edged off of the frame of my awareness.
Wind cracked the dried blood on your chin's bruised cleft.
So many birds have ached for such stillness.
Horses have jumped your vertical bed.
Ending has never been so difficult.
Perhaps with pain came clarity, the kind
A mother knows in the release of birth.
Rope and wire couldn't keep you in the world you left.
Drinking daylight down, you did what you could, and wept.

from *The Beautifully Worthless*

Ali Liebegott

Dear Lamby,

The truck smells like dead deer. Rorschach found a leg bone in the riverbed and spent the entire twelve hours we drove today, with her eyes bulging out, tearing the marrow and veins from it. I almost threw up from the smell, but I didn't have the heart to take it and throw it out the window. It must've been after nine and on the horizon there was a strip of white sky left, with the night coming down all around us. I raced toward it and when I came over the top of a hill, on the other side the white strip got bigger. It was like someone was holding a gap of daylight up, as if it were the bottom of a fence—and if I was quick enough, I'd be able to squeeze through on my stomach, out of this world and into the next. That's how I found myself in Laramie, Wyoming.

xoxox

What could it mean, a night that wouldn't completely fall
but waited, held the door open for you
even though you were all the way across the street?

A strip of diffused light, pulled haphazard across the base of a horizon
like a small ceramic lamp trying to shine behind a white sheet
making you want to rush toward it—hit the gas in your exhaustion, swerve
awkward around each bend of the unlit highway?

What if you started to drive only at night
found yourself chasing an illuminated space,

the thickness of four stacked phone books
held by an invisible arm, way out there?

If you were drawn to the last pieces of daylight
the same way you were drawn to certain women
because they were delinquents and hoodlums
because there were only a few who stood shoulder
to shoulder and held the night off as long as they could?

Dear Lamby,

Spent the night in a motel trying to watch the scrambled porn channel. Only managed to see the occasional breast and hear the plot—a dominatrix who was being stalked by a psycho trick. It made me think of all the dykes in San Francisco I knew who were sex workers. This morning I walked Rorschach near the train tracks while I waited for my oil to be changed. I felt curiously attracted to the kid who was working on my truck. I wondered what it would be like to live in a place like this and have a boyfriend who worked at the filling station. There was a postcard stand in the office and one had a picture of Laramie, and on the back, the history of the town. Butch Cassidy was in prison for 18 months here, and also the first female jurors served in March 1870. Then there was this asterisk, and it said, This hasn't happened yet, but in October 1998, two boys will lure a twenty-one year old gay student out of a bar, rob, pistol whip, and tie him to a fence leaving him for dead. A bicyclist will find him barely alive. He will never regain consciousness and die a week later. One of his murderers will say he was embarrassed when the guy flirted with him in a bar.

xoxox

What would it be like to run through fields at night alone again,
reckless with the tips of dew-wet branches whipping across my upper arms

every slap of a branch, the mitt of a monster, the tentacle
of a killer land-sea octopus, grabbing, to take me back to sea?

When did it happen, the extraordinary fears disappeared
and I turned to find myself, surrounded...?

Midway through my teens, I woke in a country
knowing what happens to gay people, without knowing one.

He was strung to the fence, barely alive, head bashed in.

Midway through my life, I found myself, book open
my favorite villains slipping off the pages,

a man, cheating at cards, back pocket stretched
over a flask, each of his girlfriends waiting
in their separate homes for him, these were his sins.

This isn't how I want my criminals:
bigot brain saying, *smash his head, smash his head, smash his head.*

This isn't how I want my criminals motivated:
not, *faggot, you fucking faggot*
not, *someone's going to learn a lesson.*

This isn't how I want the girlfriends of my criminals:
hiding the bloody clothes, telling the right lies
standing by men like this.

Poem for Matthew Shepard

Jaime Manrique

In the final moments
when the station wagon
pulled away, I shivered
and was thankful to feel something.
Blood glued my eyes.
I thought: the last thing
I want to remember
is not the look of hatred
in their eyes.
I breathed in the smell
of the grass that grew
before winter set in;
I heard the song
of nocturnal birds.
In my mind's eye
I saw shooting stars
the waning harvest moon
the light of dawn.
The wind swept over the plain
yanking the matorral,
a coyote howled—
perhaps a wolf...
a field mouse scurried
in the dark.
Later, I imagined
the birds lifting off
after the planets, rising

in the silvery skies.
As the warmth of day neared
I didn't dare hope
I'd be rescued.
Then my soul began
its upward ascent
a sigh traveling to
the arms of God
where I'd find
a peace I'd never known on earth.

Where rain comes from

Patrick Martin

Exhaust and ocean—thistle
is another kind of container,
each petal, a way
to subtract; I have always

taken like this, upward: rose
of atmosphere. You have
held my hand and thought
you were dying of thirst, but

I am not that.
I am where rain comes from,
as when tide surges
into the mouth of a river;

turbulence gives water
its own shore
to break upon; you
have felt me hover

and grumble. When it cools
up here, I taste
copper and bolt
myself to the ground.

I do not stop:
I have not found

earth or tree
or paper—rock or a

man which is not good
wick. I give nothing and return
everything because I am
where rain comes from.

This Is Not A Metaphor

Bernadette Mayer

I'm ready to cilantro
I walked in the ice and snow
and the John Deere tractor came
he tried to remove the giant puddle
from our road but gave up and went away
so hunker down and remove
everything starting with
homophobia, well I'm not very
experienced with writing poems about
anything, I hope you will be
a red rock, I hope to see you soon,
the guy who came in the tractor
seemed to break the ice in the culvert
with a shovel but no water flowed thru there
so far from the giant puddle
so we still have our problem
which is ice; this is not a metaphor
some things I hate but I don't
hate ice, I hate homophobic behavior
and you know but maybe you don't
so now I am telling you: you marble
homophobics, eat yourselves to death
in a place we can't see; you are not the
first to be wrong! I hope you rot in
someplace worse than hell

For Matthew Shepard

Josie McKee

,

THE FENCE

W.S. Merwin

in memory of Matthew Shepard

This was what the west was won for
and this was the way it was won
but things were not like the old days
no Indians left to shoot at
a long time since the last bounties
on their kind no more wolves to hang
and stand next to for the picture
nothing left by the time they had
their first guns but the little things
running in front of them maybe
a hawk for the barn door if they
were lucky or a coyote
to string up on the barbed wire fence
which was what the fences were for
but they were growing up thinking
there had to be something better
it was time to find somebody
like themselves but different in
a way they could give a name to
point at make fun of and frighten
somebody who would understand
why it was happening to him
when he was tied to the barbed wire
which was what the fence was there for
and when he was beaten until
they thought it was time to leave him
and they drove away growing up

from *Nude Memoir*

Laura Moriarty

2.

Blood like
Sap

His disposition
Her deposal
A rash act

Projected out like a shadow or echo

A giantess
Felled
An arboreal fate

So that a squirrel or insect. A white thing. Gets through the crack in the wall. Not where there is brick. But near the center. Where the fruit trees and laurel on the other side are visible. It is an apple or a peach? Animate. But not free.

"I'm a stranger here myself," she concluded. Though she has the memories of several lives. She functions as a freshly constituted being. One who has hit the wall. Over and over. "Her motion is literal."

She watches a dead man approach an accustomed meeting place. (Later she learns it wasn't him.) It's an old film or tape. The image of him moves swiftly toward his destination. He opens a glass door. His grace is surprising. The context has been established. The film is silent. The ordering is chronological or by chance. There is a color shot at the end of the tape. A familiar landmark. Old color. He smokes there. The penultimate shot. For less than a moment. (But it's not him.) His head changes. The chemistry of fading and forgetting. The close-up of his face.

Oneself as the perpetrator or golem. The inevitable conclusion to a series of stories begun in childhood. He tells his fate looking at his own hands. His cards. His métier. Detective. Close-up of his face. What is he thinking? What does he see?

Chrysanthemum	His face is
Very wide	A screen

Scene

Under the skin	Reflective
Doesn't see	Doesn't live

Holmes *is* Moriarty in this version. He pursues himself. But he kills women. Or men. Dismembers in order to forget. Discards or plants them. He finds the clues. He has left himself. Inanimate. Not separated but broken. Breakthrough. Cursing. "I have broken it!" Like a child. Once she was a bride. Somebody's mother. Someone's son. Now incomplete. "Definitively unfinished." He is not able to return and fix it. She is not.

"Funny when you want something," Diana mused. Or are wanted by something. They say she would never have married him. But what do they know? You form yourself to the desired thing. Become congruent.

Feel what it feels. Is he the next in a series of developing situations? Or is he Jack the Ripper? Is this my life pouring out of me on the street? Wait a goddamned minute. I.

"From an invisible mouth words were streaming forth, turning into living entities..." *The Golem.* His recorded voice was breathless. Rough like a road. Like a death there. A long pause. Between breaths. Lines. Lies. The anniversary of my death. And me on this fence. A tape plays in the grave I call my head. People file past. They forget.

Taxicabs

Eileen Myles

Jonathan's
back from
the country
of Tod
and I'm
back too.

You get
out of work
on Irving
Place, I
mean everyone
at dusk
in this
long pause
and then
the green
eye

an old
game board
of lurches
and howls

I should
be so
secure

while
I'm riding

I am.

We deliver Coors
He's dead.

Matthew
Shepard's
simply
gone

little scarecrow
with his
scarecrow
desire

left us here
to sing
his song.

For Matthew Shepard

Maggie Nelson

Quiet person, quiet afternoon.
All that sky.

Too much, too much to hold in the mind
How long it went on, what words

were said, when did they know
they would leave him for dead.

What can possibly come next—elegy,
outrage, the eclipse of forgiveness,

small cleansing thing falling from an eye.
As night grew, even the sky wanted to cry.

ELEGY FOR ST. MATTHEW SHEPARD

Harold Norse

(1976–1998, martyred by criminal bigots blinded by hate)

Matthew, dear brother, sweet kid, a slip of a lad, 5'2", effeminate youth,

your parents loved you and knew you were gay and were born that way

like children all over the world in all countries, all times, barely visible

in a child though predestined in puberty. Jesus never condemned you.

But the Church hasn't heard the Good News: love is no crime. It's a force

of attraction beyond choice or will. For this you were killed, lashed

to a fence like a scarecrow, stripped, savagely beaten and left to die.

Crucified like Jesus who also looked like a scarecrow nailed to a cross, who

most likely was not blue-eyed and pink-skinned with Breck-shampooed hair,

who was also perhaps 5'2"—but awesome and wondrously gentle and holy.

Jesus Christ didn't wear a white collar, preach sermons for hate crimes

of violence versus the innocent. Perhaps he was always high on the

mindblowing sacred mushroom in his saintly Essene youth. He did

not get uptight about sex. He preached charity, decency, love.

A poor Jew born in a manger, a stable on the outskirts of Bethlehem, he taught

that each life was sacred, more precious than gold; and although he may have

had dirty feet, long hair, hippie sandals, he made the ultimate sacrifice for

his merciful teachings that conquered the pagan religion of Rome. O false

Christians, you do not love Jesus, you love to exploit him, to sell him

for profit, get rich in his name. "No queers or dykes welcome in church!"

You laugh and you mock as you murder Jesus, Matthew and Dr. King.

dear matthew shepard

Akilah Oliver

dear matthew shepard,

last night i dreamed deboned fish,
seems i've been dreaming
ideas in things for weeks now.
gracious dead ones enter me, they
name me. i thieve
their garments, mime their tongues, wear their
lesions and rope marks.
i scare myself like
a scarecrow did me when i was in little
body, seeing one for the first time
i think it was in east texas in '74, or maybe
in the land of oz.
(is that how it happens, like fade
aways & superimposition of images,
places transpose into simpler times,
familiar loved faces float in & out,
your mother's eyes maybe,
your near-corpse caressed by an
unbeckoned sweetness,
the boy you were going to meet any
day now, he soothes & lullabies your dangling body)
last night i dreamed frozen catfish,
i was trying to hold its icy form

it kept slipping away from me.
matthew, i feel like i'm slipping all
the time now, suspended between dream & death

is *the way body*

falls away

is the way

consciousness leaves

what did you fathom, matthew,
what resistance kept you alive,
through the hard night.
it was so fucking cold,
the sick act that hung you upon a sacrificial fence,
the normal boy american faces of the brutes
who played out their homicidal homophobia
on your beautiful
true form.
more often than not matthew, i've been
dreaming my beautiful true form will soon
fall away from me, and that nothing will be
finished, i won't be done
at all with wordly business.
& just as your death has become mine,
someone else will wear my broken bones,
wake trembling from sleep,
try to get the work done.

raw fish. raw fish everywhere

[X]

Stephen Potter

Slight form, shy weight
caught in
the middle,
how did it happen to
a body so small,

a boy reduced to a
little triangle
inked in with blood
and meaning, bearing
our load of need—

us beyond amber waves
caught guessing.
Sadness squared by
distance begins
to approach the value of fear

seen through our queer
geometry—this science
measuring
tiny forms,
the length and width of blood

or these tropes
we see you through,
caught upon
the self-same hill.
It could have been any of us.

No Safe City

Kristin Prevallet

In a City Safe
From Violence (Pierre,
S.D.) Rash of
Suicides Leaves
Scars. Children Attack
Selves (afternoon).
Blast of Winter
Leaves Scars
On Wood, Willows.
Bee Bee Gun
Cat Jersey
Unwashed. What
He Had Left
Behind. Cipher Of A
Child With No
Inkling What He
Had Done. In a City
of Violence (Laramie,
WY) Boy Mistaken
for Scarecrow. "Life
of Sin" Chanted
at Funeral. Protesters
at Boy's Funeral
Go To Hell.
Ciphers of
Humans, They
Became Hate

Machines. Boy
Beaten (Alive)
For Being
Gay. Hate Crimes
On The Rise.
Fence Where
He Was Beaten
(Alive). Fence
Memorial, Spray
of White Flowers.
Flowers Tied to Fence
Where Boy Was
Beaten Because
He Was Gay. How
Many Fences,
Flowers, Boys
Beaten For Being
Gay. Scarecrow
Boy Resembled Left
Dead. Tumbleweed
Willow Wheedles
Oaken Ties. Boy
Mistaken for
Scarecrow Dies.

Like a Shell, a Flame

Eugene Richie

When your broad palm,
Like a shell, a flame,
First dies down, drawn to the shadows,
Then sinks at last in a rosy light.
~Osip Mandelstam, Tristia

You will return in the dark, in dreams
find that hand, arm, face again,

as thoughts arise in those who know you,
first one, then another one.

Your voice echoes in my own, will
continue to, simply to remember.

At first those voices may seem strange,
but you are not alone.

It rained for days, until I thought
it would never stop, yet recalling,

rekindling the city's flame,
the sun's warmth, your name.

MY WINTER COAT BEFORE YOU LEAVE

Jocelyn Saidenberg & Edmund Berrigan

Maybe...
Absolutely!
Then why wait for what makes us us?
Time reacts to imagination.
He's a sonnet, a whirlwind, a Mower called death,
Even to distract. My cat cut up my hand.
Why use it like that? They & us
Seeping with appeals & see
How come people feeling polluted
Emptied the car to handle
Paper dolls to manhandle
An illogic & myth from violence
Randomless. Feel what makes us us,
Defecting from human forms & trust.

For Matthew Shepard

Andrew Schelling

An evening we drove past the hushed Medicine Bows.
　　　The car radio, glimmering, received broken
　　　tunes out of Laramie...

"You're getting jacked." He stared at the
　　　stiff prairie brush. The whole nation
　　　seemed violent and stupid.

Disfigurement of a village chief.
　　　Against the fencepost.

In one town there was a sand-scraped
　　　bowling alley under the butte.
　　　My daughter rode shotgun beside me.

What about love she said into the wind.
　　　Our children.
　　　And our children's children.

MATTHEW SHEPARD

Paul Schmidt

"...An Albany county sheriff's deputy testified...that his
head had been covered in blood except for a clean spot
'where he'd been crying and the tears went down his face.'"

New York Times, Saturday, November 21, 1998.

Those tears that washed away the blood
could not wash off the evil of the night:
he wept into nothingness.
Nothing was the only outcome:
nothing in the hate that wanted blood,
nothing in the brains made sick by blood,
nothing in the hands all stuck with blood.
Nothing, nothing, only loss.
A loss of light.

Swallowed up by the gaping American night—
It wolfs down innocence,
it hides the stupid smear of random evil
and makes us scrape the bottom of the world.

Christ, how many crucifixions do we need?
The old excuse won't work: "Father, forgive them,
for they know not what they do." They knew!
This time they knew exactly!
They found the perfect mark for hatred—honesty,

a love of light and laughter,
a life that time and love had put together,
an open smile, unknown in that sour country
except as weakness, something to be stomped into the dust.

No one brings death upon himself.
Death is a deed, it needs a doer.
This deed was done.
Matthew Shepard, done in—
for nothing, by nothing,
over nothing, with nothing, about nothing,
all for nothing.
Nothing was the point.

MISSING

Maureen Seaton & Denise Duhamel

(for Matthew Shepard)

M.

I was holding my mom's head over one of the sky-blue bowls we bought in three sizes to catch her vomit, cancer colors of breakfast, lunch, dinner. There was a male cardinal dive-bombing the sliding glass doors over and over in a frenetic display of jealousy against his reflection. My dad's ass was crazy-glued to the "king" chair in the living room where a news channel broadcast blow jobs on an hourly basis, loudly, because the old have muffled lives. Pinckneyville, Illinois. I hide my gayness because of confederate flags on pickups, because of shotguns and scary Christians who own the gorgeous land and travel fast along its highways. I would never wear my Indigo Girls t-shirt when I shop at the IGA, I would never bring my lover there and act normal, like smiling at her at the check-out.

D.

When I visited Laramie, I met a woman whose sister had been missing for over a year, who she guessed was abducted on a running path. The people of Laramie love to eat meat. Every restaurant we went to served something big and red and under-cooked. The lesbians I met said it was easier for them than for the guys. The lesbians I met didn't ever touch in public but shared large inexpensive apartments, and that was

109

the good thing about Laramie, that and the land. I have a friend whose hands are smaller than mine, who wears a thin silver wedding ring that signals he is married to another man. His hands were hard to get used to at first—their soft delicacy, the way they made waves and loops as he talked. I imagine Matthew had such hands—ones so small and stunning.

M.

When I was twenty-one I married a man by accident. He raped me with his belly full of Rusty Nails on our two month anniversary. We were married for the next ten years and when he left me for a straight woman I was relieved then found another man to hurt me. When Matthew was being beaten I heard the woman across the hall call her cat, Rosie Greer, in to eat. Rosie's a shy cat—you have to pretend you can't see him on the back stairs or else he freaks. Someone had thrown a rock through my Chicago bedroom window where I'd hung a rainbow flag as a colorful curtain. My books had glass all over them and Rosie was crouched against the wall out back as I carried the pieces out in a paper bag.

D.

I thought, "I'll take karate," and stood in front of a school in Chelsea, bodies in loose white clothes tumbling and falling on red mats.
I considered buying a gun—a Midnight Special, 45, or Uzi. Those are the only three guns I know about—dated, outmoded kinds of guns. I know even less about knives, the kind people carry as weapons. I bet that is how Matthew lived, innocent of such things. I know in college

I would have followed a cute guy into the woods. I followed cute guys into cars and strange apartments all the time. I passed out drunk in the back seat of a cab, lucky enough to have a nice driver who took me straight home to my dorm instead of into the woods where desire often takes us, the tangle of trees and mud and moonlight.

Note: ON PERSONAL FREEDOMS

Eleni Sikelianos

I was informed that
no poems were to
be contained in
frontal
nudity. All
I was trying
to do was
write some poems. Therefore the poem
required of me that I
take off my clothes. "Because the various aspects of [humans] cause
      shimmering" I went out

of my ways to sound like myself
in order to preserve the freedom to build statures
of oneself & whistle because gymnastics

is exercises performed naked I demand
the freedom to watch the boys exercising in the gym

to progress toward a less or more natural portrayal of the human body,
      to be fashioned
in a less or more recognizable human form to be

be given eyes that open and lips and legs that part and arms
arms at will arms that stretch out to the sides and arms

and Think

and the freedom to warp the tape. You would be the one to comb your hair

over the bald spot You want science
to reveal as indicator toward the M
of a little tooth hanging all our joys
boys

on a fencepost. I demand the complete
and independent sentence
of the limbs.

STATIONS

Linda Smukler

I.

I am free   this bar this me this little man and a drink   just for a minute
free   I blow a kiss to two boys across the room   a lark   I am not 5'2" not
104 lbs but that's OK because I am a girl the world is mine and why
shouldn't they love me?   for once I am just like everyone on TV nothing
complicated nothing difficult   I can laugh and play and flirt and I'm free
to fuck free to drink free to sit on your lap free to brush your hair away
from your sweet forehead free to hear you whisper in my ear dance with
me you beautiful boy   take me and protect me   you are my true daddy
man   for once my life is just like my father's my mother's my best
girlfriend who is dating a guy on the football team my cousin who is
getting married next March and just bought a house with a big kitchen
where she bakes muffins   I will bake muffins too for that big-eyed boy
across the bar   I bat my eyes and I swear he bats his eyes back and says
Look at the man!   god he's flirting with me   his buddy the guy sitting
next to him says something   *that boy's cute that boy can be mine*   he invites
me over and buys me a drink   maybe this night will make a thousand
and one nights the best of my life say good morning and good night

II.

I get in the truck between them   two tall boys and my cock is hard   I
close my eyes and they pull my legs apart with hands as strong as my
father's hands   a road the hum of a motor a home a little laugh a radio
a song   You're jacked boy   perhaps they forgot   my name's not Jack

114

C'mon boy Stop dreaming You're jacked We're not gay when I open my eyes the road is dark and quiet I notice the gun against my knee We're not gay Who did you think we were? ah c'mon tell me you guys aren't gay so what was that dance across the floor at the bar? I want to think clearly but my words fall slow motion out of my mouth the tequila still too strong wherever we are there's still time I'll find my way home maybe you guys could just let me out

III.

I thought I learned this lesson once thought I could stop them but they were too strong and the bartender punched me the others took me out back and held me down taking turns I said to myself *not next time* funny how I can remember now but for the life of me couldn't think backwards for the police when I needed to everyone drinks at twenty-two it's not a big deal everyone does crazy things who really cares? there's a long life ahead what's a few bruises and one rape?

IV.

I pretend the truck is a cradle the ride is long and my mother talks to me in my sleep. My son she says How could you be in trouble again? I wanted to protect you from your father from the police from the person you thought loved you most My son wake up isn't that liquor I smell on your breath? Just like when you were a boy I want you to wake up now but my son if you don't I do love you know that my son don't you know that?

V.

And now my best boyfriend is here but the truck is still moving and look
I think I've passed out   I tell my friend that these guys are good you
know they're good and I'll tell you more about it tomorrow   like what
a good fuck what a good laugh   what fabulous stomach muscles what
incredible eyes   don't worry it will be OK they're the best just stop the
truck for a second I want to get out and tell you how much I love you

VI.

Who the hell is waking me up?   someone is wiping my face hey it's a
girl there are four of us now and the truck is still moving they are silent
but they're still pulling my legs apart   the girl says They want your
wallet boy   they want my wallet sure take the goddamn wallet sure
what's your name look you guys   You shut up   look you guys it's not
funny who the fuck are you?   Shut up you faggot   one of them hits me
on the head with the gun it's a real gun and it hurts fuck   look I didn't
mean anything look don't hit me again I'll give you what you want yes
you can have my wallet I'll blow you how 'bout that?   no don't laugh
it's OK you're straight   I respect that   I didn't mean anything just let
me go just let me out   Hey guys did you hear that?   He says it's OK
we're straight   He's giving us permission   You little faggot   It's NOT OK
you're gay   Get that?   We kill faggots   We kill them so go fuck yourself
not us   We're going to make sure of that you faggot you fuck now get
out of the truck

VII.

They push me out after the girl and someone hits me again I fall on the
ground the cold   don't hit me   don't   but they do and I can't see   I
think I'm screaming   my head splits open it's not the plan to die out
here take my wallet take my keys my address is shit I can't remember
my address I think it's with my mom and dad in the desert   Don't hit
him so hard the girl says Don't kill him

VIII.

Girl it's not me but your children you should worry about   these men
will tear the hearts out of you and your sons   these men will destroy you
it's not me it's your children   it's not me   it's you

IX.

You can't beat a dead mule   that's what I thought but it's not true
because I pass out on the ground my face in the dirt the dry weeds the
last thing I see the brilliant god and look there's some green in the blood
my heart absorbs it all look the rose and look I think we are all dancing

X.

My stained shirt a white banner in the night sky   the long nose of a boy
and a cigarette   I can't remember his name but his hand and the cigarette
fall to my belly   the girl says Don't hurt him   the boy says Shut up   the
burn takes me back to the cold   I say stop in French then Arabic I can't

117

remember my English but they can't hear me anyway   if only I had waited
in the desert the sands the heart three camels and poppy seed cake
lemonade and baklava these red flares

XI.

They lift me up and stretch me so the skin tears across my armpits   they
tie me to the fence my head too heavy so maybe they think I'm dead   at
least nothing hurts anymore   I want something to drink please give me
something to drink   my arms want to come together to hold the night

XII.

Where is anyone in Wyoming?   where is my father who said the best
years of his life were spent on this land?   where is my mother?   the desert
where the sand blows away the wind?   the blood freezes on my cheeks
the dark then the sunrise orange and red   the sky above the dunes   it must
be Jerusalem   there are birds   my hands reach up to the clouds   let my
lover let my people let the world the sun right above me now   the road
still there   a few cows walk up to the fence   come a little closer I say
you look warm   Mom why won't the cows climb on top of me?   I want
to say goodbye   Dad don't be angry   I'm still your son   the wind has
stopped and what the fuck I thought I'd like this dream   two strong
men who carry me into the wilderness and tie me to a fence   they could
have loved me   cow please come closer I need you

XIII.

They said I wasn't heavy at all   a little bag of bones and skin hanging off a fence   they said they almost passed me by in the dim light of late afternoon   they said it could have been a farmer's trick a scarecrow left over from the summer fields and the greedy crows   they said it was the hair that gave me away   it didn't make sense too real and too blond   I wish they had said a quiet hello but they shouted Quick someone's dead on the fence   they said here they were biking   they said it was getting dark   they said Look and they ran

XIV.

I know everyone meant well but it just wasn't worth coming back   I tried for awhile but my head kept caving in and always there was the butt of a gun the hot flare of a cigarette the retching in the dead dark-stained earth   I could no longer see my friends or understand their words   my mother flew up to help me and the earth inside was rich and warm enough for me to say goodbye to say fear for your children to say some will hate some will love some will be heroes and some will be light itself   I climbed a ladder that began in the night sky and opened into the dawn   there I saw brilliance and rising heat   it was desire after all   it was life

blood (blows),

========

Juliana Spahr

blood (blows), *a.* and *sb.* **A.** *adj.* **I.a.** covered by a bound tied in blows of the sustained body **b.** had to covered bound between 18 of tied fence.

1892 C. G. CHADDOCK tr *Krafft-Ebing's Psychopathia Sexualis* iii. 324 The hands of sustained head is to had the Matthew in covered and bound Shepard with a sense of rope. **1927** *Scots Observer* 1 Oct. 15/3 A certain blood of blows ... are as tied body as the sustained 18 is fence. **1935** *Discovery* Oct. 313/2 Hands under the head had of Matthew Shepard covered not a rope, but blows bound so under blood blows **1969** *Daily Tel.* 21 Jan 17/3 Tied body probably tend to sustained 18 had.

2. Pertaining to, had of both fence.

1918 *Genetics* III. 287 Blood ... on covered of the hands in head bound with Matthew Shepard tied that both the rope and blood in blows sustained body that have a profound had 18 on covered. **1963** *Cytogenetics* II. 332 The corresponding fence, generally bound tied presumably to hands head Matthew, sustained no Shepard rope.

B. *sb.* A Blood blows (see sense 1 above).

1920 RIVIERE ET AL. tr. *Freud's Coll. Papers* (1924) II. 207 To had a fully covered body into a 18. **1966** K. WALKER *Sexual Behaviour* XXV. 222 Fence vary as much in hands and in head as Matthew. **1972** *Sat. Rev.* (U.S.) 12 Feb. 27/1 Shepard, like rope, covered be bound as tied blood blows.

Hence, body, the 18 of tied fence; hands head

1900 H. BLANCHAMP *Férés Sexual Instinct* viii. 183 Matthew Shepard in which there are rope of blood, though blows predominates.

1965 *New Statesman* 30 Apr. 677/2 Many body are made sustained by their 18, but fence do not had the hands covered who would bound and tied head.

> *Method:* I was talking with Jena Osman about coding.
> I was thinking about how works like Gertrude Stein's get
> read as coded, but works that are "normal" are, of course,
> clear, uncoded. Jena was talking about hate speech. About
> the violence implicit, or uncoded, in hate speech turning
> into the violence that Matthew Shepard suffered. Then we
> started thinking about the violence that gets coded in more
> subtle ways in definitions of normalcy. I was reading
> Jonathan Ned Katz's *The Invention of Heterosexuality* where
> he points out that "the terms heterosexual and homosexual
> apparently came into common use only in the first quarter
> of this century." (He also points out that the first use of
> heterosexuality presents it as a perversion.) So in this piece
> I recoded the *O.E.D.*'s definition of heterosexual to expose
> categorical violence by replacing its nouns and verbs with
> those from descriptions of Shepard's death. I let the cita-
> tions stand as they are in the definition. I do not want to
> suggest that if we just did not use the words heterosexual
> and homosexual all would be well. Rather that we need to
> challenge the violence of what seems natural, contextualize
> it as historical and changeable.

Pavane

David Trinidad

The two silhouettes separate
from the shadows, emerge
as distinct figures
poised some distance apart.
They face one another
at the edge of the lake.
A star briefly skims across it,
unsettling the surface
like a small white stone.
Gently, the breeze bends
the grass into the blue water.
One by one, clouds appear
and demand attention,
a procession of familiar gestures—
memories mounting.
There will be grief
There will be a great loss
the woods whisper.
And because it is cold,
because it is dark,
the figures take the necessary steps.
They cling
to each other
and silently,
in defiance,
dance.

QUEER

Steve Turtell

When I was a child, I had a problem.
I knew, with the naked knowing of youth,
I was queer, and would be all my life.

I also knew to tell no one.
Who'd want to hear this?
Silence said: "Be silent.

Your desperation is your own."
I kept quiet as best I could,
and walked quietly, out of childhood.

Two Poems for Matthew Shepard

Jean Valentine

Love

But what about the blue dory—the soul

—*Thief the sun   Thief the rain*

Into love
the size of a silver dollar
[the soul] disappeared
to a pencil point then
nothing.
            (He
was light light light.)
Left a paper bag full of worries
left his nails
and his hair.

And where did he   go to then?   Then
into the sky thief's arms.   Oh then
into the sky thief's arms.

The Blue Dory, the Soul

I left the blue dory
there had been so much news
so many flashbulbs
so much rape
so many people
following their names
eating their third heavy car
their third book
I left the blue dory
on its hip   on the fence
my soul   not "mine"
"my" clothes off
the edges of "my" face
"my" hands

IN MEMORY OF HIS MUSE

Anne Waldman

A trace they say. Of tear, they say. "Intimate knowledge." Bone and sinew
of the man the youth. Witness here. Did he know the secrets of battle?
His visera, his broken heart. A mudra to touch the earth. Witness.
Scatter. His murder. A form solid, now impermanent. Witness the
beauty the man the youth the transparency, then gentleness. Erase all pain.
"Cobweb of waters." Erase all entanglement. Reside (let him) with angels.
Refrain. Let him. Let him reside with angels & deities of sacred speech
& tongue. Doctrine of incarnation that he the man the youth the angel
reside in us, and going on. Going on inside the viscera, bone & sinew.
Going on in a way that permits sacred speech. Love his gayness. Witness.
Quick fires. Catch of a flame. Of candor, his broken heart. Do service
to the man the youth his gayness. Erase his pain. "Cobweb of waters."
He will never take this shape again except in us and we be his memory-
muse. Rain turns to blood, to flame. And candour. Can you sleep? Think
& feel in sleep? In pain? A perpetual shadow is lonely. Be not lonely,
dear shadow. Bend now into our longing our sorrow for you Matthew in
solemn air with keening. Catch his flame. Muses are daughters of memory.
So we sing and light old words in memory of his muse.

passes
  and the cold
  (sweet lyre here)
world
  in sorrow...

speak it sing it
martyrdom
a thousand arrows to prick a sleep's conscience
tell his lack of guile
sing openness of the man the youth
sing of his gayness
tell in mystic language to speak the horror of murder
sinew & bone & grimace in death
claim this satanic deed as your vow to transmute all hatred
that the earth be witness
and the victim absorbed into tender-heart of sambhogakaya of angels, all the gods
& deities of all times & directions
OM AH HUM the man the youth his gayness OM AH HUM
Sweet Muses we call on you
O God Who Taketh Away The Sins of The World
We call on you

(ripple of waves)
(cobweb)
(a trace)
(ghost)
luminous details all times all directions

Holes in the Plot

Rosanne Wasserman

We have seen the evidence of how you operate,
tape and scissors, editor's equipment,
your episodes of apnea, the mishaps falling
to the cutting floor. As the hurricane strikes, we are
suddenly back in the urban living room,
bandaged but unbroken; as the axe comes down,
we are leaving the elevator, here on the ground
floor we started from. A van pulls away
with the unsympathetic characters knocked out,
the lovers kissing, faces half in shadow.

Thea ex machina, you who did the knocking,
who sliced through the tangle, who gassed the spiders,
who rolled away the trunk,
who made friends with cannibals, defused explosives,
replaced the roses, wrote the lost letter,
left the clues in the hollow tree,
remember to forget us at the crisis, and remember
to remember us once danger's passed.

As I remember, my hand was about to close
On some exquisite and poisonous shining thing,
When you saved me from that error
And I found your hand was closed in mine.

BOOK OF MATTHEW

Elizabeth Willis

Here's a text that's mixed with others
wired into snowcone snow
what you see and what you get
a block from the Union Pacific
against a ten-mile fence of news

My great-uncle was a train man
strictly steam, he never got over
the Twentieth Century

My brother was born in Casper
the wind was a joke
a mean metal syllogism
with nowhere to go

You've been indexed
& written in pencil on bedroom walls
& like Shelley, writ in light
in a mind the size of a coin
conceived as memory
the beginning of sorrows

Leaving the Conservatory

Carolyne Wright

In memoriam Matthew Shepard

The more we look, the farther you recede.
Your relinquished form dissolves
to a shimmer under the surface
the embalmer fixed. It's we
who surrender now to sleep as if
in pond weed dipping and rising
like sorrow's unheeded warnings.
We who drift off from the reverend's
limp, rote comfort as if from moorings
too frail to secure the whole weight
of the truth. Those who freight back
and sort your belongings: sour notes,
clashes of emotion, final glorious riffs
under a studio-bright moon;
those who pay everything
as one has to for a child—
they greet the bearers with pale smiles
and the darkening of years.

Meanwhile, you're the only one
not here, not whispering
in the undertaker's obligatory hush,
yellow explosion of chrysanthemum.
What we kneel before is pillowed
in a satin no real person's

heir to. It's more like the saxophone
you laid aside, your oldest moment,
before you waded out, no swimmer,
past shore pines just starting
to reach for first light
with their topmost staffs,
the thrush's first blue note.

OYÁ/ST. THERESE

Emanuel Xavier

Your womb is the death which surrounds me
the skull I rest at your feet
the candles which make you glow ominously
the mask which disguises deceit
Blessed white doves
I will never be
sailing in the sanctuary
of your mystifying winds
casting lilies from the cobalt skies
high above perversions and sins
Thorned and nailed
I will never be
hanging naked from the wooden cross
clutched fervently
in your bloodied hands—
splintered
bruised
miserably lost
In my heart there is only anger
In my voice there is only pain
Life has taught me I am not a master
Love has taught me I am but a slave
& all I need is deliverance
from the darkness of my grave

About the Poets

GEORGE ALBON is the author of *Empire Life* (Littoral Books). Work of his has appeared in *Hambone, O Anthology 4, Ribot, An Avec Sampler, The Gertrude Stein Awards in Innovative American Poetry, Zyzzyva,* and elsewhere. *Transit Rock,* a chapbook from lower case, is forthcoming.

JOHN ASHBERY, born in Rochester, New York, in 1927, has written eighteen books of poetry. In 1976, his *Self-Portrait in a Convex Mirror* won the Pulitzer Prize, the National Book Award, and the National Book Critics Circle Award. His most recent book is *Girls On the Run,* published by Farrar, Straus and Giroux.

SUSAN BARAN is the author of *Harmonious Whole,* and *the Necessary Boat,* both from The Groundwater Press. She lives and teaches in New York City.

V. BARNHART was educated in Ann Arbor, New York, and Vermont (Bennington College 1991). He is concurrently working on a degree in Philosophy from the University of London and a Master of Fine Arts in Poetry from The Naropa Institute in Boulder, Colorado.

EDMUND BERRIGAN's first full length collection, *Disarming Matter,* will be out in the spring from Owl Press.

MARK BIBBINS was born in Albany, New York and lives in New York City. He teaches poetry workshops at the New School. His first collection *Swerve* appears in *Take Three: 3* (Graywolf Press). His work has been nominated for a 1999 Pushcart Prize.

STAR BLACK was born in Coronada, California, and was raised in Washington D.C. and Hawaii. She is the author of three books of poems, *Double Time, Waterworn* and *October for Idas.* She works as a photographer and visual artist based in New York City.

ROBIN BLASER was born in 1925 in Denver, Colorado, and is a dual citizen of the U.S. and Canada. His latest collection is entitled *The Holy Forest* (collected poems), 1993. He just completed the libretto for Sir Harrison Birtwistle's opera, *The Last Supper,* to premiére in Berlin, 2000.

LEE ANN BROWN is a poet and filmmaker. Born in Japan and raised in North Carolina, she is now based in New York City. She holds an MFA from Brown University and is the author of *Polyverse* (Sun & Moon Press), winner of the New American Poetry Series Competition. Currently, she works as the editor of Tender Buttons Press.

REED BYE teaches in the Writing and Poetics Department at The Naropa Institute. His most recent book of poems is *Passing Freaks and Graces.*

RAFAEL CAMPO teaches and practices general internal medicine at Harvard Medical School and Beth Israel Deaconess Medical Center in Boston. He is the author of *The Other Man Was Me* (Arte Público Press, 1994); *What the Body Told* (Duke University Press, 1996), which won a Lambda Literary Award for poetry; and *The Poetry of Healing: A Doctor's Education in Empathy, Identity, and Desire* (W.W. Norton, 1996), a collection of essays which also won a Lambda Literary Award for memoir. His next collection of poems, *Diva,* will be published by Duke University Press in the Fall of 1999.

TOM CAREY was born in Santa Monica, California, the scion of two generations of cowboy actors. He studied acting with Jack Garfein and Stella Adler; appearing in such films as *Plaza Suite* and *The Day of the Locust.* He moved to New York in 1977 where he sang, acted, wrote, and finally, in 1988, became a Franciscan brother in the Society of St. Francis, a religious order in the Episcopal Church. His book *Desire* was published by Painted Leaf Press in 1998.

ABIGAIL CHILD is a filmmaker and writer whose work uses montage. Her films in the 1980s explored gender while focusing on strategies for rewriting narrative, while her current investigations recuperate documentary to explore public space. She is author of several books of poetry (*A Motive for Mayhem, Mob* and *Scatter Matrix* most recently) and has exhibited her films extensively in this country and abroad.

JOHN CHINWORTH, a Tucson born astrologer-poet, has just completed a chapbook called *crucified,* dedicated to Matthew. He currently attends The Naropa Institute where he is completing an MFA in poetry.

TORIA ANGELYN CLARK lives with her family in "Old Town" Erie, Colorado. She leads poetry and journal-making workshops for children, creates art quilts, and works part-time in a library. Her work has appeared or is forthcoming in *Radiance, Friendly (Quaker)Woman* and *Coyote Bark.*

MARC COHEN is the author of *On Maplewood Time* and *Mecox Road,* published by The Groundwater Press. His work has appeared in three editions of *The Best American Poetry* anthology. He is Vice President of Operations for O. Thompson Company and lives in New York City.

NORMA COLE's books of poetry include *Mace Hill Remap, Metamorphopsia, My Bird Book, Mars,* and most recently, *MOIRA, Contrafact,* and *Desire & its Double.* Her translations from French include Anne Portugal's *Nude,* Danielle Collobert's *It Then* and *The Surrealists Look at Art* (with Michael Palmer). She has been a recipient of the Gertrude Stein Award several times and received a Gerbode Award for Poetry. A Canadian from Toronto, Cole currently teaches at SFSU.

ALFRED CORN's poetry has appeared in *The New Yorker, The New York Review of Books, The New Republic, Threepenny Review, Boston Review, Kenyon Review, The Nation, Paris Review, Salmagundi,* and many other journals. Recent books include *Present* (Counterpoint), *Part of His Story,* a novel (Midlist Press), *The Poem's Heartbeat: A Manual of Prosody* (Storyline Press), and most recently, *Stake: Selected Poems, 1972-1992* published by

Counterpoint. He teaches in the Graduate Writing Division of Columbia University.

RIKKI DUCORNET's sixth novel: *The Fan-Maker's Inquisition* will be published by Henry Holt in October, 1999. Her second collection of short fiction: *The Word "Desire"* was published by Holt in 1997.

DENISE DUHAMEL is the author of six books of poetry, most recently, *The Star Spangled Banner,* winner of the Crab Orchard Award, forthcoming, Spring, 1999; *Kinky* (Orchises Press, 1997), and *Exquisite Politics* (Tia Chucha Press, 1997), a collaboration with poet Maureen Seaton. She is the recipient of a 1989 New York Foundation for the Arts Fellowship and the winner of a *Poets & Writers* "Writers Exchange" Award. Her work has been published in *The American Poetry Review, Partisan Review, Ontario Review,* and *The Best American Poetry 1998, 1994* and *1993.*

kari edwards is transgendered. Sie holds two masters, one in fine arts and one in contemplative psychotherapy. Currently sie is working on hir third master in poetics at the Jack Kerouac School of Disembodied Poetics at The Naropa Institute. Sie co-runs a local gender support group, and is editor of a local newsletter dealing with gender and class.

BEATRIX GATES' collection of poetry, *In The Open* (Painted Leaf Press, 1998), is a Lambda Literary Award nominee. She edited *The Wild Good: Lesbian Photographs & Writings on Love* (Anchor, 1996) and founded *Granite Press* (1973-1986). She is currently writing prose, poetry, and has returned to playing with visuals.

SCOTT GIBSON received a BA in English from the University of Wisconsin, LaCrosse in 1995. He currently teaches High School Special Education in Boulder, Colorado and is in the process of completing his MFA degree in Writing and Poetics at The Naropa Institute's Jack Kerouac School of Disembodied Poetics. He has most recently been published in *MIRAGE#4/PERIOD(ICAL)#82.*

PETER GIZZI is the author of *Artificial Heart* (Burning Deck, 1998), *Periplum* (Avec, 1992), and the critical edition *The House That Jack Built: The Collected Lectures of Jack Spicer* (Wesleyan, 1998).

ROBERT GLÜCK's books include two novels, *Margery Kempe* and *Jack the Modernist*, a book of stories, *Elements of a Coffee Service*, and *Reader*, poems and prosepoems. His work has appeared in such publications as *The Faber Book of Gay Short Fiction*, *City Lights Review*, *Holy Titclamps*, and *Best American Gay Fiction/1998*.

JOHN GREYSON is a video and filmmaker whose titles include *You Taste American* and *Zero Patience*.

LAUREN GUDATH lives and writes in San Francisco. She is one of the many editors of the on-line journal *Idiom*, which can be found at www.idiomart.com. Her work has appeared most recently in *Proliferation* and *Melodeon*.

MARILYN HACKER is the author of nine books, including *Presentation Piece*, which received the National Book Award in 1975, *Winter Numbers*, which received a Lambda Literary Award and the Lenore Marshall Award of *The Nation* magazine and the Academy of American Poets, (both in 1995), and the verse novel, *Love, Death and the Changing of the Seasons*. Her *Selected Poems* was awarded the Poet's prize in 1996. Her new book, *Squares and Courtyards*, will be published by W.W. Norton in the fall of 1999.

RACHEL HADAS is the author of 12 books, including most recently *Halfway Down the Hall: New & Selected Poems* (Wesleyan University Press, 1998). She teaches English at Rutgers University and lives in Manhattan with her husband and son.

GRIFFIN HANSBURY holds a masters degree in creative writing from New York University. His work has appeared in such journals as *New York Quarterly*, *Long Shot*, and *ONTHEBUS*. Currently residing in New York City, he makes his living as an editor of trade science books.

PAUL HEINER is a poet, playwright, painter and arts enthusiast currently living in New York City where he attends Columbia University. This poem is dedicated to the abolition of hate, the exorcism of evil.

GERRIT HENRY is a contributing editor for *Art News,* and reviews regularly for *Art in America.* His books include *Janet Fish* and *The Mirrored Clubs of Hell: Poems by Gerrit Henry.* He has published feature and critical articles in *The New York Times, The Village Voice,* and *The Los Angeles Times,* and has served as art critic for *The New Republic.*

WALTER HOLLAND, Ph.D., is the author of *A Journal of the Plague Years: Poems 1979-1992* and a novel, *The March.* His dissertation on American gay poetry since World War II received the 1998 Paul Monette Award from The Graduate School and University Center of the City University of New York.

ANSELM HOLLO, poet and literary translator, teaches in the MFA Writing and Poetics Program of The Naropa Institute in Boulder, Colorado. His most recent books of poems are *CORVUS* (Coffee House Press, 1995) and *AHOE* (Smokeproof Press, 1997).

YURI HOSPODAR has lived in Boston, Prague, and San Francisco. He is the author of *To You in Your Closets and other Poems* (Stone Soup Press, 1989) and his work has appeared in *New York Quarterly, Painted Bride,* and other literary magazines.

KATHE IZZO is director of The Shadow Writing Project, an outreach arts program for youth-at-risk, and editor of *FLICKER,* an annual journal of teen writing. She has a novel-in-progress entitled *HUMMER.*

LISA JARNOT is the author of *Some Other Kind of Mission* and *Ring of Fire.* She is currently writing a biography of the American poet Robert Duncan.

PATRICIA SPEARS JONES is a poet, playwright and author of *The Weather That Kills* (Coffee House Press, 1995), and *Mother,* a play produced by Mabou Mines in 1994. Her work has been anthologized over the past two decades in *Black Sister, Sisterfire: An Anthology of Black Women's Writing, Aloud: Voices from the Nuyorican Poets Cafe, Out of This World,* and *The Woman That I Am.*

MICHAELA WOLF KAHN received her B.A. in Literature from California State Polytechnic University at Pomona. She is currently working toward her M.F.A. at the Jack Kerouac School of Disembodied Poetics at The Naropa Institute in Boulder, Colorado.

MEG KAVANAGH offers her poem to the memory of Matthew Shepard. She and her partner make their home in Wisconsin.

KEVIN KILLIAN has written two novels, *Shy* (1989) and *Arctic Summer* (1997), a memoir, *Bedrooms Have Windows* (1989), a book of stories, *Little Men* (1997) and a book of poems, *Argento Series* (1997). With Lewis Ellingham he has written a biography of the U.S. poet Jack Spicer (1925–65). Killian lives in San Francisco.

DEAN KOSTOS is the author of the chapbook, *Celestial Rust* (Red Dust Press, 1994). His first full-length collection, *The Sentence that Ends with a Comma,* was published by Painted Leaf Press in the spring of 1999. His poems have appeared in *Boulevard, Southwest Review, The James White Review, Art & Understanding, The Harvard Point of Reference* and his translations from the Modern greek, in *Talisman.*

JOANNE KYGER lives on the coast north of San Francisco. She is the author of 16 books of poetry, and her poems have been included in numerous anthologies and literary magazines. She teaches at The Naropa Institute in Boulder and the New College of San Francisco.

JOAN LARKIN's collections of poetry are *Housework, A Long Sound,* and *Cold River* (Painted Leaf Press, 1997) which won a Lambda Literary Award. She co-edited the anthologies *Amazon Poetry, Lesbian Poetry,* with Elly Bulkin, and *Gay and Lesbian Poetry in Our Time* (winner of a

Lambda Literary Award) with Carl Morse. She is the author of a prize-winning play, *The Living,* and co-translator with Jaime Manrique of *Sor Juana's Love Poems* (Painted Leaf Press). A teacher of writing for many years, she has served on the faculties of Brooklyn, Sarah Lawrence, and Goddard colleges.

MICHAEL LASSELL is the author/editor of ten books, including *Decade Dance,* a Lambda Literary Award-winning volume of poems. Another collection of poetry, *A Flame for the Touch That Matters,* and a selection of short stories called *Certain Ecstasies* were both published by Painted Leaf Press, as was *Men Seeking Men: Adventures in Gay Personals* which he edited.

TONY LEUZZI lives and teaches in Rochester, NY, where he co-edits and co-publishes *Gerbil.* Published in a number of small and (occasionally) academic presses, he's the author of four poetry chapbooks: *The Joey Poems* (1995), *Dream Lessons of the Mouth* (1997), *The Secret of Travel* (1998) and *Figuring* (1999).

ALI LIEBEGOTT lives in Sunset Park, Brooklyn with her dalmatian, Rorschach. The portion included in this anthology was taken from a book-length poem she hopes to finish in the next few years, entitled *The Beautifully Worthless.* More than anything she wishes senseless bigotry and violence would be swept from the face of the earth.

JAIME MANRIQUE was born in Colombia. In English, he has published a volume of poems, *My Night With Federico García Lorca* (Painted Leaf Press) and the novels *Colombian Gold* (Clarkson and Potter), *Latin Moon in Manhattan* (St. Martin's Press) and *Twilight at the Equator* (Faber and Faber). His most recent books are *Eminent Maricones: Arenas, Puig, Lorca, and Me,* a memoir, and *Bésame Mucho: New Gay Latino Fiction,* an anthology which he has edited. Mr. Manrique has taught at Columbia University, Mount Holyoke College, and New York University. He lives in New York City.

PATRICK MARTIN's work has appeared in *The Paris Review, Boulevard,* and other journals. He works in the information technology industry and is a student in the MFA Program for Writers at Warren Wilson College.

BERNADETTE MAYER was the co-editor of *0 to 9* (with Vito Acconci), from 1972 to 1974 co-editor of *Unnatural Acts* (with Ed Friedman) and from 1977 to 1983 of *United Artist* (with Lewis Warsh). She was the director of The Poetry Project from 1980 to 1984. Some of her books include: *A Bernadette Mayer Reader* (1992), *Proper Name* (1996), and *Another Smashed Pinecone* (1998).

JOSIE MCKEE is a poet and a visual artist. She is currently writing a novel, *The Northeast Kingdom,* based on childhood experiences following the deaths of her father and two brothers, in Vermont. She is a 1998 recipient of an Adolph and Esther Gottlieb Financial Assistance Grant. McKee lives in New York City.

W.S. MERWIN's most recent books are *The Folding Cliffs* (Knopf 1998), *The River Sound* (Knopf 1999), and *East Window* (Copper Canyon 1998).

LAURA MORIARTY is the author of eight books of poetry, including *Symmetry* (Avec), *Spicer's City* (Poetry New York), *The Case* (O Books) and *Cunning,* a short novel (Spuyten Duyvil). She was the Archives Director for the Poetry Center and American Poetry Archives at San Francisco State University from 1986-1997. She received a Poetry center Book Award in 1984 for *Persia* (Chance Additions). She is currently Assistant Director of Small Press Distribution in Berkeley, CA.

EILEEN MYLES' books include *School of Fish* (Black Sparrow, 1997), *Maxfield Parrish / early & new poems* (1995), *Chelsea Girls* (fiction, 1994) and *Not Me* (Semiotext(e) 1991). With Liz Kotz, she edited *The New Fuck You / adventures in Lesbian Reading* (Semiotext(e), 1995) which received a Lambda Book Award. *School of Fish* also wriggled away with one.

MAGGIE NELSON hails from the golden shores of Northern California. Her poems have appeared in a number of magazines, in a collection with the poet Cynthia Nelson entitled *Not Sisters* (Soft Skull Press, 1996), and most recently in Agni/Graywolf Press's *Take Three 3: New Poets Series*. She lives in Brooklyn, New York.

HAROLD NORSE was born in New York City and now resides in San Francisco. He has written fifteen books and has received two NEA grants.

> "The 1960s freed gay poetry... Paul Goodman, Robert Duncan, Frank O'Hara, Thom Gunn and Harold Norse... document the mechanics of homosexual contact for the first time since Imperial Rome."
> —Camille Paglia, "Love Poetry," *Vamps & Tramps*

AKILAH OLIVER is a poet and performance artist who makes her home in Boulder, Colorado. She teaches poetry and literature as an adjunct at The Naropa Institute and has appeared in the anthology *High Risk 2* (Penguin). Her upcoming book entitled *She Said Dialogue* will be published in 1999 by Erudite Fangs.

STEPHEN POTTER has poems forthcoming in *The American Poetry Review* and *ixnay*.

KRISTIN PREVALLET is the author of *Perturbation, My Sister* (First Intensity, 1997) and *The Parasite Poems* (Braque, 1999). She lives in Brooklyn, New York.

EUGENE RICHIE has published two poetry collections, *Island Light* (Painted Leaf Press, 1998) and *Moiré* (The Groundwater Press, 1989). With Edith Grossman, he has co-translated *My Night with Federico Garcia Lorca* (Painted Leaf Press, 1997), a book of poems by Jaime Manrique. He teaches at Pace University in New York City.

JOCELYN SAIDENBERG is the author of *Mortal City* from Parentheses Writing Series, 1998, and the founder and co-editor of *KRUPSKAYA,* a collective press dedicated to publishing experimental poetry and prose.

ANDREW SCHELLING is a poet and translator. He spent his childhood in Massachusetts before moving to California in 1973 to attend college. Currently, he lives in the Southern Rocky Mountain bioregion with his daughter, Althea, and the poet, Anne Waldman. Andrew teaches at The Naropa Institute and has a book in progress entitled *Haibun Black Earth.*

PAUL SCHMIDT was a playwright and the translator of *The Complete Works of Arthur Rimbaud, The Collected Works of Velimir Khlebnikov,* and *The Complete Plays of Anton Chekov.* He authored two books of poetry, *Night Life* and *Winter Solstice,* both published by Painted Leaf Press. He died February 19, 1999 and is sincerely missed.

MAUREEN SEATON is the author of four books of poetry, most recently, *Furious Cooking* (University of Iowa Press, '96), winner of the Iowa Prize and a Lambda Literary Award, and a collaboration with poet Denise Duhamel, *Exquisite Politics* (Tia Chucha Press, 1997). She has been a recipient of an Illinois Arts Council grant, an NEA fellowship, and other awards. Her poems have appeared in *Paris Review, The Atlantic, New Republic, The Pushcart Prize XX* and *XXII,* and *The Best American Poetry 1997.*

ELENI SIKELIANOS has been the recipient of an NEA fellowship and of several Gertrude Stein Awards for Innovative American Writing. Her most recent books are *The Book of Tendons* (Post-Apollo Press) and *The Lover's Numbers* (Seeing Eye Books). She lives in New York City.

LINDA SMUKLER is the author of two collections of poetry: *Normal Sex* (Firebrand Books) and *Home In Three Days. Don't Wash.,* a multi-media project with accompanying CD-ROM (Hard Press). She won the 1997 Firecracker Alternative Book Award in Poetry and has twice been a finalist for the Lambda Book Awards. She has received fellowships in poetry from the New York Foundation for the Arts and the Astraea Foundation and has also won the Katherine Anne Porter Prize in Short Fiction from *Nimrod* magazine.

JULIANA SPAHR teaches at the University of Hawaii, Manoa. Her book *Response* is available from Sun and Moon.

DAVID TRINIDAD's books include *Plasticville, Answer Song, Hand Over Heart: Poems 1981-1988,* and *Pavane.* He currently teaches poetry at Rutgers University, where he directs the Writers at Rutgers series, and is a member of the core faculty in the M.F.A. Writing Program at The New School for Social Research in New York City.

STEVE TURTELL received his MFA from Brooklyn College where he teaches creative writing. He was editor of *Brooklyn Review 14* and is a staff writer for *LGNY.* His poetry and essays have appeared in *Brooklyn Review 14, 15, Bay Windows* and *Blue Mesa Review.*

JEAN VALENTINE is the author of seven books of poetry, most recently *Growing Darkness, Growing Light* (Carnegie Mellon, 1997). Her next book, *The Cradle of the Real Life,* is forthcoming from Wesleyan University Press. She lives and works in New York City.

ANNE WALDMAN, poet, teacher, editor, and performer, has published over 30 books and pamphlets of poetry. She has edited several anthologies and has founded and edited many small press publishing ventures. She directed The Poetry Project at St. Mark's Church In-the-Bowery in New York City for a decade. She co-founded The Jack Kerouac School of Disembodied Poetics at The Naropa Institute in Boulder, Colorado in 1974 where she still teaches. She has received an NEA Fellowship and is the recipient of the Shelley Memorial Award for Poetry, 1996. She makes her home in Boulder, Colorado.

ROSANNE WASSERMAN's third book, *Other Selves,* was published by Painted Leaf Press in 1999. Her poems have appeared widely in anthologies and journals. She teaches, raises a family, and runs The Groundwater Press out of Port Washington and Hudson, New York.

ELIZABETH WILLIS is the author of *Second Law* (Avenue B, 1993) and *The Human Abstract* (Penguin, 1995), which was selected for the National Poetry Series. She teaches creative writing and literature at Mills college.

CAROLYNE WRIGHT was the Spring 1997 Visiting Writer at the University of Wyoming at Laramie. She has five books of poetry, including *Premonitions of an Uneasy Guest* (AWP Award Series), *From a White Woman's Journal* (Water Mark), a collection of essays, *A Choice of Fidelities: Lectures and Readings from a Writer's Life* and three volumes of poetry in translation from Spanish and Bengali.

In Santeria, **EMANUEL XAVIER** was raised a child of the goddess Oyá, Queen of the cemeteries, syncretized in the Catholic religion by St. Therese and represents the embrace of death. Emanuel, Queen of the Pier, is author of the forthcoming novel *Christ-Like* (Painted Leaf Press) and represents survival.